"*Compelled* is pure gold. Dudley Rutherford insightfully helps us overcome fear and engage with others in a loving way while pointing them to their greatest need—the mercy and forgiveness of God."

Jud Wilhite

Author of *Pursued* and senior pastor of Central Church

"Dudley Rutherford's faith in Jesus and amazing and genuine way of sharing the gospel is something of complete joy. Once again he has created a must-read—and his labor of love is a true call to action that helps us all spread the joy of the gospel!"

Adam Housley, Emmy Award–winning journalist, former MLB player

Tamera Mowry-Housley, Actress, author, talk show host

"Dudley Rutherford has simplified the call of God and clarified the commission of Christ. In a clear, sensitive, and practical manner Rutherford declares: you can do it!"

Dr. Kenneth C. Ulmer

The King's University and Faithful Central Bible Church, Los Angeles, CA

"Believers have been called to take part in the Great Commission of sharing Jesus Christ with the world, and Dudley Rutherford provides both the motivation and the blueprint for you to become a confident, grace-filled soul winner."

Mark Jackson

Pastor, ESPN analyst, and former NBA player and coach

"*Compelled* is not theoretical; it is practical and practiced. Long before I was challenged by Dudley Rutherford's words in this book, I was challenged by Dudley's example in everyday life. This book will give you the courage and confidence to share Jesus everywhere you go."

Kyle Idleman

Teaching pastor, Southeast Christian Church, Louisville, KY

"Dudley Rutherford gets back to the basics of how to share the gospel and why it matters. You'll be convicted, empowered, and inspired."

Phil Cooke, Ph.D.

Filmmaker, media consultant, and author of *The Way Back*

"So many books talk about stewarding our finances, but *Compelled* is about stewarding our hope. Dudley Rutherford believes the gospel is the hope of every man. Read and digest his wisdom and passion, and you'll start investing hope in those who need Jesus!"

Rick Atchley

Senior teaching minister, The Hills Church, Richland Hills, TX

"An engaging and inspiring book on how to share your faith with those around you. *Compelled* is rich in experience, deep in insight, and encouraging in tone. A truly welcome book on evangelism!"

Reverend Canon J. John

Author, speaker, and founder and director of Philo Trust, UK

"Dudley Rutherford is an incredible communicator and influential leader who practices what he preaches. *Compelled* will motivate you to faithfully open your mouth rather than fearfully remain silent."

Dave Stone

Pastor, Southeast Christian Church, Louisville, KY

"*Compelled* offers overwhelming motivation and practical tools to do what God has called every believer to do: participate in the amazing process of leading people to salvation."

Miles McPherson

Pastor of Rock Church, San Diego, author, and former NFL player

"Pastor Dudley reminds us that gratitude for our personal experience of God's grace, forgiveness, and healing should compel us to tell others how they can find relief from the agony of defeat through Jesus Christ."

Dr. Jerry Taylor

Assistant professor of Bible, Abilene Christian University

Stevie Moriah

Tell The World!

Compelled

The Irresistible Call to Share Your Faith

[signature: Dudley Rutherford]

DUDLEY RUTHERFORD

Tell Everyone about Christ
Love
II COR 5:14 —

WORTHY®
PUBLISHING

Compelled: The Irresistible Call to Share Your Faith
Copyright © 2018 by Dudley Rutherford

Published by Worthy Books, an imprint of Worthy Publishing Group, a division of Worthy Media, Inc., One Franklin Park, 6100 Tower Circle, Suite 210, Franklin, TN 37067. WORTHY is a registered trademark of Worthy Media, Inc.

HELPING PEOPLE EXPERIENCE THE HEART OF GOD

eBook available wherever digital books are sold.

Library of Congress Cataloging-in-Publication Data

Names: Rutherford, Dudley, author.
Title: Compelled : The Irresistible Call to Share Your Faith / by Dudley Rutherford.
Description: Franklin, TN : Worthy Publishing, 2018.
Identifiers: LCCN 2017054500 | ISBN 9781683972518 (tradepaper)
Subjects: LCSH: Witness bearing (Christianity)
Classification: LCC BV4520 .R88 2018 | DDC 248/.5—dc23
LC record available at https://lccn.loc.gov/2017054500

Unless otherwise noted, Scripture quotations are taken from the Holy Bible, New International Version®, NIV®. Copyright © 1973, 1978, 1984, 2011 by Biblica, Inc.™ Used by permission of Zondervan. All rights reserved worldwide. www.zondervan.com. The "NIV" and "New International Version" are trademarks registered in the United States Patent and Trademark Office by Biblica, Inc.™ | Scripture quotations marked NJKV are taken from the New King James Version®. Copyright © 1982 by Thomas Nelson. Used by permission. All rights reserved. | Scripture quotations marked AMP are taken from the Amplified® Bible, Copyright © 1954, 1958, 1962, 1964, 1965, 1987 by The Lockman Foundation. Used by permission. (www.Lockman.org) | Scripture quotations marked by ESV are taken from the ESV® Bible (The Holy Bible, English Standard Version®), copyright © 2001 by Crossway, a publishing ministry of Good News Publishers. Used by permission. All rights reserved. | Scripture quotations marked NLT are taken from the Holy Bible, New Living Translation, copyright © 1996, 2004, 2007 by Tyndale House Foundation. Used by permission of Tyndale House Publishers, Inc., Carol Stream, Illinois 60188. All rights reserved. | *Italics in Scripture quotations have been added by the author for emphasis.*

For foreign and subsidiary rights, contact rights@worthypublishing.com

Published in association with Don Gates of the literary agency The Gates Group, www.the-gates-group.com.

ISBN: 978-1-68397-251-8

Cover Design: Matt Smartt, Smartt Guys Design
Interior Design and Typesetting: Bart Dawson

Printed in the United States of America
18 19 20 21 22 23 BPI 8 7 6 5 4 3 2

This book is dedicated to the
intensely loyal staff at Shepherd Church,
who work every day to reach
the city of Los Angeles and the world
around us for Jesus Christ.

Contents

CHAPTER 1

A Once-in-a-Lifetime Opportunity

"The Church exists for nothing else
but to draw men into Christ....
God became man for no other purpose."

C. S. LEWIS

It was a beautiful night at Dodger Stadium. Loyal fans sporting their team apparel formed a patchwork of blue and white across the multilevel stands. Above, the stadium lights sparkled like diamonds against the near-black sky. Below, not a blade of grass was out of place on the baseball field. And the Dodgers were up by two. Everything seemed perfect.

I was sitting behind third base next to a preacher friend of mine named Ron. He had flown into town, and I was thankful to spend a few hours catching up with him while we watched America's pastime. Sitting next to Ron was a kid around the age of twelve, who I realized right away was completely blind.

To this day, that boy is one of the greatest pictures of faith I've ever seen.

The entire game he had his baseball glove on with his hand outstretched toward the field. His mother sat next to him, and during every play, she leaned over to the boy's ear and quietly explained what was taking place.

"That was a hit to right field."

"The pitcher just struck out the batter."

"That was a double play."

Throughout the entire game, the mother described every pitch and every play for her son. And throughout the entire game, the boy sat with his glove out as though he was going to catch a fly ball.

In about the fourth or fifth inning, something surprising happened. Just like that, a foul ball popped up and headed precisely in my direction! I looked up and thought, *Man, this ball is coming straight at me!*

What happened next, for a moment, seemed extraordinary at least and miraculous at best. I don't know if it was the spin on the ball, the wind, or the Holy Spirit, but as that ball began its downward trajectory, it started to move away from me and toward the blind boy sitting patiently with his baseball glove wide open.

My first thought was *not* that it might land in his glove. That wasn't even a possibility as far as I was concerned. My thought was, *That ball is gonna hit that boy in the head! It's gonna kill him!* Thankfully, the baseball flew over his head, missing him by an inch, and landed in the next row. In an instant, four or five guys scrambled down on the floor, fighting for the baseball. During the scuffle, the ball rolled way down the aisle until a lady picked it up.

The guys were still fighting for it, so I said, "Guys, guys! She's got the ball over there!"

They looked up and there was this woman, happy as a clam, with the baseball in her hand. She put the ball away and continued to watch the rest of the game.

The whole scene bothered me. In my opinion, the ball didn't end up with the right person. After a couple of innings went by, I leaned over to my preacher friend and said, "You know what? I'm going to go ask that lady if she'll give me the ball so I can give it to that kid."

Ron said, "No, no, no, let me ask her."

And I said, "No, no, no, no, let me ask her."

He said, "No, let me ask her."

"Okay," I relented.

As Ron stood up, I said, "Hey! Before you go, here's a twenty-dollar bill. If she won't give it to you, offer her that twenty bucks, and if you wanna give her twenty bucks of your own, that'll be forty. I bet she'll give it to you for forty dollars."

I handed him my twenty and went upstairs to get a Coke. When I returned, Ron was sitting there with a dejected look on his face.

"What's wrong?" I asked him.

"She wouldn't give it to me," he replied.

"What happened?" I asked.

"Well, I went over there," Ron began, "and I said, 'Ma'am, you see that kid over there? He's twelve years old. He's totally blind, and he's been sitting there the *entire* game with his baseball glove. Is there any way you would give me that baseball so I could give it to that kid?' She said, 'No.'"

Ron continued, "So then I took out the forty dollars and I said, 'I'll give you forty dollars for that baseball.' And she said, 'Okay,' and she started to hand me the ball. But her boyfriend reached out and grabbed her hand and said, 'No. This is a once-in-a-lifetime opportunity, to go to a Dodgers game and get a foul ball. We're not giving it to the kid.'"

Now, I know I'm a preacher, and preachers are supposed to

have good thoughts about other people. But when Ron told me what happened, I did not have good thoughts.

I wanted to turn around and say to the couple, "Do you wanna know what a once-in-a-lifetime opportunity is? It is *not* going to a Dodgers game and having a foul ball roll right over to you out of nowhere—and you just look down, pick it up, and take that baseball home. That is not a once-in-a-lifetime opportunity."

> When we walk closely with Jesus, He gives us a clearer vision. We become more like Him, and we begin to notice people.

I wanted to say, "A once-in-a-lifetime opportunity is going to a Dodgers game and having a foul ball roll right over to you out of nowhere, and you reach down and pick it up. Then you look over, and you see a twelve-year-old kid who has never seen anything in his entire life, let alone a baseball, and yet he's sitting there in faith, believing that he's going to catch a fly ball. And you take that baseball and you go over there, and you stick it in that kid's glove and you say, 'Here you go, kid. Here's a baseball.' Now that's a once-in-a-lifetime opportunity."

A Clearer Vision

What happened that night at Dodger Stadium is a remarkable picture of the gospel and what we choose to do with it once we receive it. Many of us are just like that couple. We're sitting somewhere minding our own business, unconcerned and unaware of spiritual matters. And all of a sudden God—who is loving beyond our wildest imagination—graciously places salvation in our hands. We weren't even anticipating it. We weren't cognizant of the fact that God was working behind the scenes, before the beginning of time, to prepare and provide a way for us to be saved.

Yet He sent Jesus to die on the cross. Christ was buried and resurrected on the third day, and once we put our faith and trust in Him, the Lord God Almighty gives us eternal life.

What do we do next with this incredible gift? Do we hand it to the next person who needs it, or do we hold on to it tightly like a brand-new foul ball at a Major League Baseball game? Are we so overcome with joy and gratitude that we can't help but share it with others, or do we keep it to ourselves and think, *I'm saved. Thank God I took advantage of a once-in-a-lifetime opportunity?*

But there are people all around us who are in need of this incomparable gift too. There are people who are lonely and broken. There are people who are depressed, hurting, and hopeless. There are people who are spiritually blind. There are people who are in bondage to sin and need to hear the gospel of Jesus Christ.

When we walk closely with Jesus, He gives us a clearer vision. We become more like Him, and we begin to notice people. Not only do we notice them, but we also start to see people as Jesus does. Our perception changes. Instead of looking at people on the surface, we realize there's more than meets the eye.

In Matthew 9:35–36, we get a glimpse into how Jesus views mankind:

> Jesus went through all the towns and villages, teaching in their synagogues, proclaiming the good news of the kingdom and healing every disease and sickness. When he saw the crowds, he had compassion on them.

Now, let's be honest. Seeing huge crowds of people usually doesn't spark compassion within us, right? If you are like me—living in a large, metropolitan community like Los Angeles, California—you are constantly surrounded by large numbers of people. Sitting on the freeway with thousands of cars crawling in front of you usually produces more frustration than compassion!

We're more likely to think, *I wish these people would get out of my way!*—not, *Gee, I wish I could tell all these people how much Jesus loves them!*

But when we examine what Jesus taught and how He lived (1 John 2:5–6), we will see people as He sees them—even in a big crowd. For the Christian, the greater number of people we encounter ought to equal greater compassion and awareness of the deep, spiritual needs of mankind. We should become compelled to tell them about the hope we have found in Jesus.

Where Are the Workers?

Matthew 9:35–38 reveals the type of people for whom Jesus had compassion: they were sick, harassed, lost, and helpless, "like sheep without a shepherd." In verse 35, His compassion turned to action when He not only healed their diseases and sicknesses (which is to serve their physical needs) but also verbally shared the good news of salvation with them (which is to meet their spiritual needs). Then He issued this edict to His disciples in verses 37–38:

> The harvest is plentiful but the workers are few. Ask the Lord of the harvest, therefore, to send out workers into his harvest field.

I've often wondered what Jesus would say about the lost people in our world today. Did you know that the population of humanity has grown from 300 million people in Jesus's day to almost 7.5 billion today?[1] Cities, towns, and villages across the globe are teeming with people who need to hear about how they can be reconciled to God through Jesus Christ. If our Lord asked two thousand years ago for workers to be sent forth into the fields that were ripe for harvest, what would His prayer be for the present-day fields that have *twenty-five times* more people than in His time?

What would He say if He saw so many sheep without a shepherd in your city, in your country, and in other nations around the world? The truth is, our planet is in desperate need of people who are compelled to share the hope of Jesus Christ. *We* are Jesus's workers—you, me, and everyone who professes the name of Christ. He is counting on us to take His message to a world that is spiritually bankrupt. Pause for a moment and silence the many distractions competing for your time and attention, and you'll hear the faint whisper. A gentle yet irresistible call in your spirit. An invitation nudging you toward something greater than you could ever imagine.

A Compelling Call

In 2 Corinthians 5:11–15, after writing about our responsibility to "persuade others" about the good news, the apostle Paul made this beautiful assertion:

> *For Christ's love compels us,* because we are convinced that one died for all, and therefore all died. And he died for all, that those who live should no longer live for themselves but for him who died for them and was raised again. (vv. 14–15)

When the New Testament was written, the word *compel* referred to the privilege Roman officials and soldiers had to force people (as well as their horses, equipment, and family members) into public service.[2] Our contemporary definition of *compel* carries the idea of driving or overpowering something or someone. It also means "to have a powerful and irresistible effect, or influence."[3] But

Paul identified that it was not Roman officials, nor force or obligation, that compels us to share the gospel with our fellow man, but Christ's love! You might say that to compel is to propel into action.

After meeting Jesus on that dusty road to Damascus, Paul's life was changed forever and set on a different course. No longer fervently persecuting the Christian church as he had done before, he literally had seen the Light. And he spent the remainder of his life traveling the known world to tell about the Light of the World (see John 8:12 and 1 Corinthians 15:8–10).

The gospel's irresistible effect is the reason why Paul went on missionary trips and voyages across tumultuous seas. His travels put him in unspeakable amounts of danger, distress, and brushes with death. But Paul could not help himself. He was compelled to tell others about the love of Christ.

In the same way, though you were once on a path away from God, you now have a miraculous story of conversion. You've met the Lord and have been changed by Him. Just as He did for Paul, God wants to put your life on a different course for His glory. When we truly examine the depth of God's love and the truth of His gospel, we will become compelled to share it with others just as Paul and so many other fearless believers have done throughout the history of the world.

This once-in-a-lifetime opportunity is not unique to Los Angeles where I live. The same is true for your city and for any city—big or small—on earth today.

The Lost in Lodz

Vance and Jennifer were living an enjoyable life in Southern California. Vance worked at a law firm as an assistant manager, and Jennifer helped to plant one of our Shepherd Church campuses in the West Valley of Los Angeles before moving to Iraq to become a church planter and an English teacher. When Jenn moved back to the United States, she and Vance got married and had a son.

The young couple had intended to move to Iraq together and even took their infant, Nathan, there for a trip to find work. They became team leaders, sold all they had, and started raising support. It was in the middle of this process that they felt increasingly uneasy about the decision and sought the Lord for more direction. Over several months, God closed the doors to Iraq and led them to Poland in 2013 instead.

Poland has a population of nearly 38.5 million people—coincidentally, almost the exact same population as the state of California. Vance, Jenn, and their son moved to Lodz, which is the third largest city in Poland. Their second son, Josiah, was born there. Not a single person in the hospital spoke English when Jenn delivered him!

Although Poland is technically a "Catholic country," less than 0.3 percent of the population is evangelical Christian.[4] There are two Jehovah's Witnesses to every evangelical—in Lodz it is more like thirty-five Jehovah's Witnesses to every evangelical. Vance and Jenn bear witness to the fact that there is a huge need for believers to share the gospel there.

Enduring extremely cold weather, the country's communistic mind-set, spiritual attack, loneliness, and occasional health issues, Vance and Jenn are filled with certainty that Poland is where God wants them to be. Just as the Holy Spirit did in my heart three decades ago, He has called Vance and Jenn to serve a people in unfamiliar territory. To bring Jesus Christ into a country that needs Him, they've left behind the comforts of family, friends, and yummy food (Jenn says there's only so much you can do with sausage and potatoes, which are plentiful in Poland).

Jenn started with a small discipleship group of four girls and

Vance started with six guys. Through the ministry that God has allowed them to begin in Lodz, there are now over fifty people who have either been discipled or are being discipled. There are now three house churches as well.

Vance and Jennifer could have looked at the country of Poland and said, "You know, there are hardly any Christians living in Poland, and that's just the way it is." Or, "There are millions of people there who have never heard the gospel, but that doesn't really have anything to do with us."

Instead of believing that the spiritual state of Poland could never change, they believed in the power of the Holy Spirit moving and working through believers throughout the world to transform hearts indiscriminately. Christ's love compelled them to abandon everything they knew to gain His heart for the lost.

Later in this book I'll share more of Vance and Jennifer's journey with you. It will encourage you greatly! Their lives demonstrate the joy that can be had, and the impact that can be made, when we choose to take seriously Jesus's words in Matthew 28:18–20, which is the mandate of our faith:

> All authority in heaven and on earth has been given to me. Therefore go and make disciples of all nations, baptizing them in the name of the Father and of the Son and of the Holy Spirit, and teaching them to obey everything I have commanded you. And surely I am with you always, to the very end of the age.

God has done truly remarkable things in Lodz through two willing vessels. And He is changing lives not just in Los Angeles, not just in Lodz, but all over the world. Yet I am convinced that there is so much more Jesus wants to do, can do, and will do when we become open to a once-in-a-lifetime opportunity. This does *not* necessarily mean that God will ask you to move to another city or country, although He sometimes does. But what I do know for sure is that God desires to change your mind-set to be open and ready to do His will, to influence those around you with truth and boldness.

No Regrets

I will never forget something an elder in our church told me right before he died. He had served the congregation faithfully for sixty years, and as his frail body prepared to step into eternity, he told me, "Dudley, one of my biggest regrets in life is that I cannot recall actually leading someone to Jesus Christ."

My heart grieved along with his. This man had knowledge of the Scriptures. He knew the Lord. He had likely sat in more than three thousand church services in his lifetime, sang worship songs, tithed, and served others. But one thing was missing: he never used what he knew to bring salvation to one person. Not one.

Friend, this does not have to be the deathbed regret of any Christian. My guess is that there is an undeniable prompting in your soul to share the life-changing message of the gospel with others. I'm so glad you are responding to it by reading this book! With every fiber of my being, I believe we serve a mighty God who invites us into a powerful partnership with Him and will equip us to do His will here on earth.

> God desires to change your mind-set to be open and ready to do His will, to influence those around you with truth and boldness.

When I look around, I see a lot of good things committed Christians are doing in the world as the hands and feet of Jesus. But I would say the majority of professed Christians are not engaging the culture as we ought to be. We are concerned with our own affairs, our careers, and our calendars. We are distracted by our phones, social media, TV, the Internet, our pets—and even cute videos of *other people's* pets. (I get it; I like adorable animals as much as the next guy!)

Instead of setting our hearts and minds on things above, we often pursue earthly things (Colossians 3:1–2). And it's so easy to do in this technologically advanced age of comforts and conveniences.

When we *do* engage the culture about the things of God, it's often in a way that is obnoxious. Or we are ill-equipped. Just look at the comments section of any article or social media post on the topic of faith. You'll see that at the first sign of opposition, timid believers begin to question what they know and become silent. Meanwhile, overzealous believers take an argumentative approach that lacks the gentleness and respect we are called to have in 1 Peter 3:15 when defending the faith.

Not to engage the culture at all, or to share God's Word in a combative or arrogant tone, are two unnecessary extremes. Yes, we are to be unashamed of the gospel (Romans 1:16). Yes, God's Spirit gives us boldness and power (2 Timothy 1:7). But our partnership with God, which beckons people to salvation, preaches in humility and love.

Hope of the World

We have the hope of the world living inside us. The most pressing crisis at hand is that there are people who are lost without Jesus—prisoners to their sin, searching for answers, lonely, hurting, confused. Some are suicidal, thinking there is no way out of the situation they're in currently. Many need healing spiritually, physically, and relationally. The message of the cross is lifesaving, and I'm convinced beyond any doubt that the best life anyone could possibly live is one that serves God and obeys His Word. This includes sharing His Word with others.

My passion is to see this current generation of believers become so compelled by the love of Christ that we cannot help but try to persuade our fellow man that He died for all. I want to see the modern-day church more closely resemble the early church, which was fearlessly and singularly focused on spreading the gospel—to the degree that the early disciples were accused of turning the world upside down by those who opposed them (Acts 17:6). With all my heart I believe that same boldness can be mustered in the church today to transform the world for Jesus!

Most likely you are reading this book because you believe that too—and I'm overjoyed and thankful for that! But perhaps when it comes to articulating your faith, you don't know where to start. Maybe you're afraid you'll say the wrong thing or that you'll get rejected. It's not always going to be easy, but if you are willing to join me on this journey, you will find that sharing your faith is the most rewarding thing you will ever experience. Through my story and through the stories of many others, you will be encouraged and equipped to take your faith to those around you without fear.

Can you begin right now by writing down, in the study question section below, five names of people you know who need Jesus? Just five people. Your list could include a relative, coworker, or friend . . . or perhaps someone you're intimidated by, or a neighbor, or someone you doubt will ever give their life to Jesus. Please take a moment to write their names below and keep these names in mind as you read this book. You can even start praying now that God will help you introduce them to the hope of the world.

Extravagant Grace

For these loved ones and acquaintances of yours, hearing the gospel is a matter of life and death. Paul explained unequivocally in Ephesians 2:1–3 that without Christ, we are dead in our transgressions and deserving of God's wrath. That's bad news—a tragic reality for everyone on this planet who has not put their faith in Jesus Christ. Now let me show you what Paul wrote in the very next few verses, because it is unfathomably good news:

> But because of his great love for us, God, who is rich in mercy, made us alive with Christ even when we were dead in transgressions—it is by grace you have been saved. And God raised us up with Christ and seated us with him in the heavenly realms in Christ Jesus, in order that in the coming ages he might show the incomparable riches of his grace, expressed in his kindness to us in Christ Jesus. (vv. 4–7)

Paul also explained this same idea more simply: "But God demonstrates his own love for us in this: While we were still sinners, Christ died for us" (Romans 5:8).

We have been saved by the excessive love, mercy, and grace of God. And since it exceeds us, we should not keep it to ourselves. The *greatest* assignment we have ever been given by Almighty God is to grab ahold of the once-in-a-lifetime opportunity in front of us—which is sharing the gospel with others before they enter into eternity.

Our God wants everyone to come to repentance (2 Peter 3:9). He "wants all people to be saved and to come to a knowledge of the truth. For there is one God and one mediator between God and mankind, the man Christ Jesus, who gave himself as a ransom for all people" (1 Timothy 2:4–6).

Through His extravagant grace, your heavenly Father has made a way for all who put their faith and trust in Jesus Christ to have everlasting life. Even the difficult coworker or the classmate who uses sarcasm or humor to mask his or her pain. The friend who seems to have it all together and is disinterested in "that Jesus stuff." The businessman consumed with chasing the next deal. The problematic teenager who won't listen. The grumpy cashier at the grocery store. The homeless person on the street begging for spare change. The PTA member who causes drama. Yes, even the family member who seems to do everything in his or her power to flee from the things of God.

Everywhere you go, people need Jesus! They need answers. They need the truth and hope, and they need a solution to life's greatest burdens.

Yet many people have never heard a clear and simple explanation of how forgiveness and redemption take place through faith in Christ alone. It's our obligation to tell them. Paul left no room for debate when he wrote,

> How can they call on him to save them unless they believe in him? And how can they believe in him if they have never heard about him? And how can they hear about him unless someone tells them? And how can they hear about him unless someone tells them? And how will anyone go and tell them without being sent? That is why the Scriptures say, "How beautiful are the feet of messengers who bring good news!" (Romans 10:14–15 NLT)

When we truly examine what the Bible says about evangelism,

I believe we will find that becoming a messenger who brings the good news is a compelling call. In fact, I think we will discover that this calling is so wonderful, so fulfilling, that it is quite irresistible. It's almost as though we have no choice but to preach the gospel.

> For when I preach the gospel, I cannot boast, since I am compelled to preach. Woe to me if I do not preach the gospel! (1 Corinthians 9:16)

Just as if a foul ball landed right at your feet, you have a once-in-a-lifetime opportunity to pick up the gospel and take it to desperate souls. No one is out of God's reach, and He uses Christ followers like you to carry His message of truth. What an incredible honor! Starting today, may you look around and truly *see* those around you, asking the Lord for the courage and the opportunity to share the good news with them.

DISCUSSION QUESTIONS

1. Write down five names of people you know personally who need Jesus. As you think about these people, what do you think the power of salvation, restoration, and redemption—through Jesus Christ's sacrifice—can do in their lives? Begin the process of praying for the people on this list regularly.

2. Read 2 Corinthians 5:11–15. According to this passage, what compels us as believers to persuade others to fear the Lord? Why does it compel us (see verses 14 and 15)?

3. How has your experience with God's love and grace compelled you to go beyond what is comfortable or comprehensible?

4. Read Matthew 9:35–38. Why do you think the workers are few when the harvest is so plentiful? What steps can you take today to become a willing and faithful worker?

5. Many of us are like the dying elder mentioned on page 11. What regrets would you have if you knew you were going to die today? How many of those on your list involve conversations with people that you haven't had yet? What do you think is stopping you from having those conversations?

CHAPTER 2

New You, New Task

"The only way the corporate body of Christ
will fulfill the mission Christ has given
it is for individual Christians to have a vision
for fulfilling that mission personally."

DR. DAVID JEREMIAH

The first time I met Dave Hopla, he was sunbathing in the backyard of a mutual friend of ours named David Pump. Hopla was balancing one of those sun reflectors on his chest, working on his tan. After Pump introduced us briefly, this thought went through my head: *That guy and I will never ever get along.*

Dave Hopla is an East Coast guy. He has an East Coast accent and an East Coast attitude.

I grew up in the Midwest, but I've pastored a church on the West Coast for nearly thirty years. It's safe to say that I've become a West Coast guy with a midwesterner's heart.

If you didn't know, East Coast people can sometimes rub West Coast people the wrong way and vice versa. They're just different from one another—like oil and water. That's exactly how it was between Dave and me. We didn't say much to each other that day, but from our limited interaction, I knew we weren't likely to become friends.

One day David Pump told me about a basketball shooting clinic that Dave Hopla was conducting at California State University, Northridge (CSUN). He told me I absolutely had to go and watch this guy coach. Dave Hopla is probably the greatest shooting instructor for basketball on the planet. He's coached countless high school, university, and NBA players. In fact, as I write this, he holds the world record for the most three-pointers made in sixty seconds.

I agreed to go to the clinic and brought along my son, Dallas, who was twelve years old at the time and already enamored with all things basketball. I knew he'd be interested in whatever this coach had to say. When we arrived at the CSUN gym, the place was humming. On the floor, young players practiced drills while coaches sat in the stands chatting with each other. As I looked around the court, I recognized multiple faces from television. Just about every big-name college basketball coach was there for the purpose of scouting and recruiting some of the best high school players in the state of California. And part of that day's events was the shooting clinic by Coach.

The court cleared as the clinic began. Dave took a basketball and stood under the net and began to shoot the basketball into the hoop. Every time he made a shot, he took a step back. While he continued to shoot the ball, he taught the kids, explaining his mechanics and his form. He kept stepping farther and farther away from the hoop, talking the whole time. To my recollection, he didn't miss a single shot. He must have made twenty shots in a row. Even from half-court, he couldn't miss.

Every jaw in that gymnasium was on the floor. The coaches

and players couldn't believe what they were seeing. Everyone was silent, including my son, listening intently to every word Dave said.

Unfortunately, many of those words were cusswords. Remember, Dave had a hard-core attitude, and that attitude came with a hard-core vocabulary. It was kind of like watching an Al Pacino movie character teach a middle school class.

Dave's language got so vulgar, I had to pull my son out of there. I was fuming. My son had never heard language like that before, and I didn't want him at his age hearing it at all. I couldn't shake my outrage, not because he had offended me, but because of the bigger picture. There were all kinds of impressionable young men in the gym that day. Some of those boys didn't have great role models growing up. And there was Dave, showing off his unbelievable skill and holding the undivided attention of every person in that room, but completely wasting the opportunity.

So I went to my office and wrote him a letter. I wrote him a *long* letter. I told Dave that he had those kids in the palm of his hand. They would have done anything he told them to do. He had an amazing opportunity: either to lead those kids down a path of good or down a path of evil. And I told him I felt he chose poorly. Next time, I explained, I hoped he would choose to lead those young men down a path of righteousness.

Expect the Unexpected

I didn't think Dave would ever respond to that letter. I thought he'd probably read it, mutter a few expletives, and toss it in the trash can on his way to his next basketball clinic. But I had to at least say what was on my heart. I felt compelled to do so.

One day David Pump called me and said, "Guess who's been going to your church."

"Who?" I asked. I didn't have the slightest clue.

"Dave Hopla."

"You're kidding," I said. I didn't believe it.

"Yeah, he's a Jesus Freak now," David said. "You know, a Bible thumper."

The next Sunday rolled around, and as I was delivering the message that morning, I looked over and saw Dave Hopla sitting in the front row with his Bible, taking notes. I was shocked. I wanted to meet with him for a few minutes after church, so I asked one of the ushers to bring him to my office.

When Dave arrived, he told me that the letter I had written had made a huge impact on his life. He actually agreed with my assertion that he was throwing away an opportunity to do some good with his gift and with his life. So Dave had turned his entire life over to the Lord, and now he intended to do something remarkable with it.

Dave has served on the staffs of multiple NBA teams and drawn rave reviews from famous players like Kobe Bryant and Ray Allen. NBA Coach George Karl referred to him as not only the greatest shooter on the planet but also the greatest shooting coach.[1] Every time Dave shows off his craft on a basketball court, every eye is on him. But what makes Dave most proud now isn't his shooting percentage or the names of players and coaches who revere him.

What makes Dave beam with joy is what he gets to say to players at the end of his clinics. He tells young men and women that they can make every shot they ever take and they can have all the talent in the world, but without Jesus they've got absolutely nothing. The gospel changed Dave's life, and now he is compelled to tell others how Jesus can change theirs as well.

Only God can bring about that kind of transformation of the heart. Dave Hopla is a new creation, and so are you. We find this truth in 2 Corinthians 5:17, which reads, "Therefore, if anyone is in Christ, the new creation has come: The old has gone, the new is here!" The word *new* in Greek is *kainos*, meaning unused, fresh, and novel.[2] This connotes a renewal of our mind, heart, and spirit, which overflows into our actions and purpose.

An Awesome Assignment

Now that you are a new creation, you have received a brand-new task in life. Jesus gave this task in Mark 16:15: "Go into all the world and preach the gospel to all creation."

Jesus said He would send those who follow Him to fish for people (Matthew 4:19). And in Matthew 28:19–20, which is often called "the Great Commission," He instructed believers to *go*, *make disciples*, *baptize*, and *teach*. This wonderful task is echoed in Jesus's last words before He ascended to heaven in Acts 1:8:

> But you will receive power when the Holy Spirit comes on you; and you will be my witnesses in Jerusalem, and in all Judea and Samaria, and to the ends of the earth.

The Bible says if we love God we will obey His commands (John 14:15, 23; 1 John 5:3), and without a doubt, one of God's commands is to preach the gospel and to be Christ's witness all over the world. We find evidence of this awesome assignment in the Old Testament as well. Just take a look at Psalm 96:2–3:

I'm not sure we will ever be able to fully grasp what a huge honor and privilege it is to be a messenger of God's truth and salvation.

> Sing to the LORD, praise his name;
> proclaim his salvation day after day.
> Declare his glory among the nations,
> his marvelous deeds among all peoples.

Can you imagine if each and every Christian would "proclaim his salvation day after day"—to "declare his glory among the nations"? If we spent less time on the distractions of this world and more time sharing "his marvelous deeds among all peoples"? Oh, I bet we could change the world!

I'm not sure we will ever be able to fully grasp what a huge honor and privilege it is to be a messenger of God's truth and salvation. And yet no one else but you, me, and the family of believers are able to take up this great task. This supernatural assignment was not assigned to supernatural beings. Have you ever wondered why?

Not for Angels

If God were to ask me, "Dudley, who do you think should carry this message of salvation to the world?" my answer would be an easy one. "Angels!" I'd say.

Why not? Angels have been used by God throughout the Bible to bring very important messages to people. In fact, the Greek word for *angel* can also mean "messenger." Look at some of the messages angels have delivered:

- An angel told Zechariah that his wife, Elizabeth, would give birth to John the Baptist, even in their old age (Luke 1:13).
- An angel told Mary she was going to conceive and bring forth a Child (Luke 1:35).
- An angel told Joseph to take Mary home as his wife even though she did not carry his child (Matthew 1:20).
- An angel warned Mary and Joseph about Herod and instructed them to leave the country (Matthew 2:13).

- Once Herod had been killed, an angel led Mary and Joseph back to Bethlehem (Matthew 2:19).
- The night sky lit up as angels pronounced the Messiah's birth to the shepherds (Luke 2:13).
- In the Old Testament, angels also took care of Elijah (1 Kings 19:5–7), mustered Gideon's courage (Judges 6), and rescued Lot from Sodom and Gomorrah (Genesis 19:1–17).

From the beginning of creation, angels have been very busy carrying God's messages. Today books are written about them, and Hollywood has even put them "in the outfield" and imagined people in crisis being "touched" by them. There's even a baseball team in Los Angeles named after them! With all of their experience and fame, it just makes sense that angels would be the obvious choice to herald the message of redemption to the world.

But think about it. How many people do you know were saved because of an angelic visitation? Probably none. And I think there are two very important reason why God has chosen *us*—not angels—to share the gospel with the world.

First, angels are busy with their own tasks. Ephesians 6:12 reveals that there is a spiritual battle going on in the heavenly realms, dark against light. God's angels are very likely involved in this battle (2 King 6:17; Jude 1:9; Revelation 7:1). Angels serve God (Psalm 103:20; Revelation 22:9). They are also busy praising and worshiping Him (Psalm 148:1–2; Isaiah 6:3; Hebrews 1:6; Revelation 5:8–13).

The second and perhaps greater reason angels are not modern-day messengers of the gospel is because angels do not have a testimony. God has chosen us, not angels, to be His ambassadors of the good news because angels have never experienced the weight or consequences of sin. They have never heard a sermon on salvation and then felt the convicting Spirit of God tugging on their hearts. An angel could never sing, "Amazing grace, how sweet the sound, that saved a wretch like me." Why? Because they have never been a "wretch." They're angels—not humans who live in a fallen world.

We, on the other hand, have a testimony and an ability to say to others, "Hey, my life used to be a wreck. I was trapped in sin just like you. Then one day I met Jesus Christ, and He changed my life. The same way He changed me, He can change you too." This is important because people tend to be more receptive to someone they can relate to—someone who has been in their shoes. This is empathy, and it serves as an amazing bridge between two people.

Jesus Christ is the ultimate example of this: "For we do not have a high priest who is unable to empathize with our weaknesses, but we have one who has been tempted in every way, just as we are—yet he did not sin" (Hebrews 4:15).

Though we are not perfect like our Savior, the sin and struggles He saved us from are all part of our testimony. Jesus said that those who have been forgiven much, love much (Luke 7:47). Because of this, I believe forgiven sinners are powerful witnesses for God's grace. David Wilkerson, the late pastor and writer, once said,

God uses people. God uses people to perform His work. He does not send angels. Angels weep over it, but God does not use angels to accomplish His purposes. He uses burdened broken-hearted weeping men and women.[3]

You and I may never be able to open up prison doors like the angels have done, or speak to prophets, or shut the mouths of lions, or ascend and descend on a ladder from heaven, or minister to Jesus in His darkest hour. But we have a song that the angels cannot sing! We have a message they are not qualified to deliver.

As much as they probably would love to, and as much as they would obey, the Bible says God has given *us*—not angels—the ministry of reconciliation.[4] God deemed it our responsibility to deliver His message to the world. You and I are called to be the spokespersons on His behalf.

Sometimes we stand in awe of professional ministers, missionaries, and spiritual giants of the Bible and church history, but every single one of those people were, at one time, ordinary. They were regular, average people who were in need of salvation. God saved them, and their lives went from ordinary to extraordinary when they chose to respond to the compelling call to share God's love and life-changing message with others.

The world is waiting to hear your testimony of God's grace! You have been transformed. Just like John Newton wrote in the timeless hymn "Amazing Grace," you once were blind, but now you see! We will talk more about the power of your testimony in a later chapter because, as a new creation, you have an important story to share with those around you.

For now, I want to share with you four important things that happen when you become a new creation in Christ as it relates to evangelism.

1. A New Creation Becomes Mission Minded

Dave Hopla is still employed as a world-renowned shooting coach. But he has also enthusiastically embraced a new task: to tell anyone who will listen about Jesus Christ his Savior. Dave will share openly that before he got saved, his bad language didn't stop at cursing; he used to be a chronic liar as well. But Christ changed that too.

There are eight panels on a basketball, and Dave writes a word on each of those eight panels: "Always tell the truth. Tell the truth always."[5] Because of his faith in Jesus Christ, he is now committed to the biblical command to "put off falsehood and speak truthfully to your neighbor, for we are all members of one body" (Ephesians 4:25). Moreover, Dave has a new mission to share the truth of the gospel both on and off the basketball court.

Oftentimes Christians think that they have to quit their jobs and go into full-time ministry in order to become involved in the important task of sharing the gospel. That may be the case for a few. But for most of us, God desires to use us right where we are to be a light, a witness, and an influence for His glory. Your job, or your school, or your home might very well be your mission field!

(Just to be perfectly clear, if you were involved in any shady form of business before you became saved, I'm not advising you to stay there. I can say without a doubt that the Lord does not want you to be involved in anything that is immoral, illegal, or disreputable.)

Starting from the book of Genesis, the Bible is filled with scriptures that encourage hard work and responsibility. Paul wrote in 1 Thessalonians 4:11–12 that we are "to make it your ambition to lead a quiet life: You should mind your own business and work with your hands, just as we told you, so that your daily life may win the respect of outsiders and so that you will not be dependent on anybody."

Did you know that there was a season in the apostle Paul's life when he actually had two jobs? Yes, even Paul—the person who wrote nearly half the books in the New Testament and was arguably one of the greatest evangelists of all time—had to have a regular "day job" outside of ministry. We learn in Acts 18:1–3 that Paul was a tentmaker and worked in that profession for a time while he was in Corinth. Verse 4 tells us how he spent his weekends: "Every Sabbath he reasoned in the synagogue, trying to persuade Jews and

Greeks." Later in verse 5, we find that when his friends Silas and Timothy arrived in Corinth from Macedonia, "Paul devoted himself exclusively to preaching, testifying to the Jews that Jesus was the Messiah."

When you become a new creation in Jesus, the Lord wants you to be mission minded no matter where you are—at your job, after work when you're running errands or with your family, and on the weekends. My encouragement would be to always serve with a godly attitude and to know that God has chosen to give you this job and this sphere of influence at this time in your life. It is a blessing to have a career and daily provision, amen? So keep your eyes open for ways to be a light and a blessing to your bosses and your coworkers. God can use you right where you are.

2. A New Creation Becomes an Ambassador

Every high school, university, and professional sports team adopts a mascot or nickname. They are carefully picked to represent the history, mission, attitude, and values of each entity. The Dallas Cowboys. The New York Yankees. The Los Angeles Lakers. The Alabama Crimson Tide. What comes to mind when you hear those names? Some team names, when spoken, generate an immediate memory or feeling.

When I was growing up and considering my college future, I was like every other young boy in our neighborhood with visions of grandeur. I could picture myself running a football down the field for the Oklahoma Sooners or shooting hoops for UCLA.

All that changed one Sunday night when I was in the ninth grade. I was sitting in the back of the church, goofing off with my buddies while my father was preaching. To this day, I don't know the main text of the sermon. I didn't hear one word of my dad's message because I simply wasn't paying attention. And my dad knew it.

During the invitation when we stood to sing, the Holy Spirit of God came over me. I don't know any other way to describe it, but I knew at that moment God was calling me into the ministry. So I walked to the front of the church. This was back in the days when the preacher had you stand and he told the entire church why you had come forward. "This is so and so," he'd say. "He's come to be baptized." And the preacher would take your confession of faith right there. Or he'd announce, "Everyone say hello to Joshua, Angie, and their daughter, Kyra. They've come to join the church."

So Dad looked at me with a bewildered expression on his face, and he said, "Why did you come forward, son?"

"Dad, I've got a calling to be a preacher," I replied. "I want to be a preacher."

I think he wanted to say, "Son, if you're going to be a preacher, you're gonna have to start listening better in church." But he didn't.

Quite frankly, I was just as surprised as my father was. As a boy growing up in a preacher's home, I'd never once heard my dad say, "Son, you'd make a very good preacher." Not once. He never said, "You ought to go to Bible college. You know, follow in your dad's footsteps." He never pushed me in that direction. It was something God did within my heart. Something I cannot explain. But the Lord used that moment in time in a young junior high kid's life to set his feet on an entirely new course.

Once I graduated from high school, I decided to attend Ozark Christian College in Joplin, Missouri. When I learned of their mascot, it served as confirmation that I made the right choice in a school. Staying true to their mission of ministry and to the basic calling for every Christian, they proudly call themselves—wait for it—the Ozark Ambassadors.

Okay, I'll admit, an Ambassador isn't as fierce as a Warrior or a Giant or an Eagle. Many people don't even know what an ambassador is or does! However, that name is essential to the students, staff, and alumni of Ozark Christian College. It speaks of something much closer to our hearts.

An ambassador represents someone greater than himself or herself. When the president of the United States meets with the Japanese ambassador, for example, he speaks with a person who represents the governing body of Japan. The ambassador does not speak and act on his own behalf, but on behalf of the leadership of his country.

As believers, we carry the title of ambassador too! Every Christian shares the responsibility of proclaiming God's message of redemption to the world. Take a look at how 2 Corinthians 5:20 explains it:

> We are therefore Christ's ambassadors, as though God were making his appeal through us. We implore you on Christ's behalf: Be reconciled to God.

Being Christ's ambassadors is not a suggestion or a recommendation—it's mandated by Scripture. Hudson Taylor, the nineteenth-century British Christian missionary to China, once stated, "The Great Commission is not an option to be considered; it is a command to be obeyed." And yet I have actually heard Christians say these words: "Hey, other people can believe what they want. That's between them and God. It's none of my business." That is not the attitude of an ambassador. It's the attitude of a wallflower.

We have a God-given responsibility to represent Christ to the world. Our marching orders come from the Creator of the entire universe! He is awesome, holy, majestic, all-knowing, ever present, and all-powerful. If we filled the earth with books stacked up to the sky, there wouldn't be enough pages to list His glorious attributes. Please let me encourage you to undergo a biblical study, if you haven't done so already, about the Lord's omniscience, omnipotence, and sovereignty. It will be one of the greatest, most humbling studies of your life.

And when we come to fully understand (as much as our human minds are able to understand) God's almighty nature, we easily submit to His authority and will for our lives as believers—just as an earthly ambassador submits to the jurisdiction of the president or ruler of his or her country. When we talk to others about Jesus, we are speaking on His behalf. We are delivering His message with His authority.

> You are an ambassador for Jesus. Commit yourself fully to this essential calling, and God will empower you to speak in ways you've never considered possible.

This reality helps remove some of the nerves that come along with sharing Christ with others. You are not speaking with your own authority and power. If you were, you probably wouldn't get too far! Instead, you are speaking with the authority and power of the Holy Spirit who lives inside you.

Always remember that you are an ambassador for Jesus. Commit yourself fully to this essential calling, and God will empower you to speak in ways you've never considered possible.

3. A New Creation Becomes Bold

When I was nineteen years old, I preached at a little church in Fayetteville, Arkansas. The church only had about forty people, most of whom were elderly. Of those forty members, only one was younger than me. I would love to say we had a youth group, but in reality, it was more like a "youth kid."

I was just starting college in Missouri, so I had to drive about two hours every weekend to get to the church. At this time I was a very shy, mild-mannered, and meek guy. I was the kind of guy who didn't want to offend anyone. People who know me now are shocked to learn this, but it's the truth.

Every time I drove to Fayetteville, I was terrified of the three elders of the church who awaited me. I referred to them as the "smoking elders" because all three of them smoked cigarettes. They burned through them by the pack. And what's worse, they actually lit them up inside the church building. (Yes, I said *inside* the church building!)

Their smoking always bothered me. I knew it was an unhealthy habit, and the fact that they were church leaders indulging in plain view of the church wasn't helping us out at all. Who wants to go to church and smell cigarettes as soon as they step in the door? Many, many times I wanted to talk to them about it, but I couldn't. They intimidated me.

One day the director of a local orphanage called me and asked if he could bring the kids to church. "Of course," I replied. "Come over and we'll have lunch for you too!"

He brought about ten kids, which increased our church attendance that Sunday by 25 percent. After the service was over, we all moved downstairs to enjoy our lunch together, but the director pulled me aside and asked to speak to me. Once we were out of sight and away from everyone else, his demeanor changed. He got right in my face and started poking me in the chest with his index finger.

Dead serious, he said, "Preacher, I'm gonna tell you something. Every single day these kids fight the temptation to drink, swear, and smoke. The last place I ever thought they would see a bad example was in the church! You better start preachin' what people need to hear and not what they want to hear."

Then he said, "We will never come back to this church again."

Though his words were harsh, they were a necessary wake-up call. For the rest of that afternoon, I was racked with conviction. My church had served as a bad example to those kids, and it was all because I didn't have the guts to say what needed to be said.

That evening, as I arrived for our Sunday-night service, I prayed earnestly for God to grant me boldness to do just what that man had said. To preach what people needed to hear.

During my prayer, I felt the power of the Holy Spirit rise up within me and fill me with courage and purpose. Before I even entered the church door, I knew I would finally be able to speak what God had placed on my heart. When I got up to preach that night, I threw away my prepared notes. I stood up there and let them have it with both barrels.

I don't remember everything I said during that message, but I do remember saying at one point, "If God had intended for you to smoke, he would have put a chimney on your head! Smoking won't send you to hell, but it will sure make you smell like you've been there!" I stressed the fact that we shouldn't be smoking in the first place, let alone inside the church of Jesus Christ, because doing so would undoubtedly set a poor example for others in the faith.

Truth be told, I was surprised at myself. I never knew I could speak like that. And many in the church were just as surprised as I was. The point being, God unleashed a boldness in me that was completely contrary to my nature.

The very next Sunday morning I made my drive from college to Fayetteville. I was preparing to deliver the message when one of the three elders pulled me to the side.

Calmly he said, "Dudley, we've decided to let you go."

"Why?" I asked.

He said, "For financial reasons."

"Financial reasons? You only pay me fifty dollars a week!"

"I know, but we just can't afford to keep you."

I tried reasoning with him, saying, "I'll tell you what—I just want to preach. What if you paid me five dollars a week? That would at least cover the gas. Would that be in the budget?"

He firmly answered, "No, we're letting you go. Today will be your last day."

I immediately felt that same boldness rise up in me again, except this time it was twice as strong. For the second service in a row, I threw my sermon notes away and let them have it. They *definitely* didn't want me to come back after that message.

I will never forget what the orphanage director said to me on that Sunday afternoon in Fayetteville: "You better start preachin' what people need to hear and not what they want to hear." If I had a photo of him digging his finger into my chest, I would have it framed and sitting on my office desk to this day. It changed my life.

Today you may be just like I was at age nineteen—timid and frightened to say what you know in your heart is true. God can empower and embolden you to proclaim truths you never thought were possible. He will change the lives of others before your very eyes.

For God has not given us a spirit of fear, but of power and of love and of a sound mind. (2 Timothy 1:7 NKJV)

You don't have to be a full-time preacher or pastor to get

involved. If you ask Him, God will instill in you a burden for sharing your faith. Just as the prophet Jeremiah proclaimed in Jeremiah 20:9, the Word of God will become like a fire in your heart and in your bones that you won't be able to hold in even if you tried.

4. A New Creation Becomes Clothed in Humility

The last thing that happens when you accept the new task given to you after becoming a new creation in Christ is quite remarkable. You get to exchange your old, dirty, raggedy clothes (representing your sin and old ways) for clean, brand-new clothes (representing your justification and sanctification through Christ). But instead of trendy styles or expensive fabrics, God's Word details what your new clothes are made of:

> Therefore, as God's chosen people, holy and dearly loved, clothe yourselves with compassion, kindness, humility, gentleness and patience. (Colossians 3:12)

As a new creation in Christ carrying out a new task for the Lord, you now are to be clothed with compassion, kindness, humility, gentleness, and patience. These qualities are worth far more than an entire closet filled with designer suits or fancy dresses. I want to focus on humility because I believe it is a huge precursor to having the boldness to share one's faith.

Where does humility come from? When we as human beings are so prone to pride and egotism, how do we cultivate true humility in our hearts? James 3:13 reveals that "humility comes from wisdom." You might be thinking, *Okay, so how do I get wisdom?* We find this answer in the book of James as well:

If any of you lacks wisdom, you should ask God, who gives generously to all without finding fault, and it will be given to you. (1:5)

It's surprisingly simple: pray for wisdom and it will be given to you—and out of that wisdom, humility springs forth. C. S. Lewis wrote in his book *Mere Christianity*, "True humility is not thinking less of yourself; it is thinking of yourself less." When we think of ourselves less, it takes away the concern for our possessions, our reputation, and our safety when we endeavor to share Jesus Christ with someone. Paul's declaration in Acts 20:22–25 is a beautiful example of this truth. He wrote,

And now, *compelled* by the Spirit, I am going to Jerusalem, not knowing what will happen to me there. I only know that in every city the Holy Spirit warns me that prison and hardships are facing me. However, I consider my life worth nothing to me; my only aim is to finish the race and complete the task the Lord Jesus has given me—the task of testifying to the good news of God's grace. Now I know that none of you among whom I have gone about preaching the kingdom will ever see me again.

After Paul spoke these words to the Ephesian elders, he got down on his knees and prayed with them as they wept. What a heart-wrenching scene! Paul said good-bye to beloved friends and fellow workers in ministry, knowing he would never see them again. The Holy Spirit revealed to him that hardships and prison awaited him. And yet he forged ahead with his God-given task, unconcerned for his own future or safety. He considered his life worth nothing; his singular mission was to share the good news. Paul is an astonishing example to us all of humility and total surrender to the Lord's will in order to bring the gospel to lost souls.

．－ — — ———— — － ．

When you become a new creation and take up the new task of sharing God's grace with everyone you meet, you will become a mission-minded ambassador who is bold and clothed in humility. You don't have to be the apostle Paul, or C. S. Lewis, or a missionary, or even a pastor like me. God has uniquely equipped you and put people in your life so that you can be a light for Him!

Moreover, it doesn't matter who you used to be. If you used to lie or use foul language like Dave Hopla once did, God will put a new message on your tongue. If you used to be shy or intimidated by others like I used to be at age nineteen, God will give you incredible courage to speak the truth. The power of the Lord Jesus Christ changed Dave; it changed me, and it has changed you. New creation, new task!

Now that we understand who we are in Christ and what we are called to do, let's explore the motivations that compel us to actually take part in this eternally significant calling.

DISCUSSION QUESTIONS

1. What set of skills do you possess that you can use to glorify God? Like Coach Hopla, how are you using the platform that God gave you to show a godly life that is appealing to others?

2. Why do you think God uses ordinary, average men and women to share His gospel rather than some extraordinary display of power or some other supernatural message?

3. What is your unique responsibility to share the testimony of who God is and His redemptive plan for all of humanity? Who are you responsible for in your role as an ambassador to God and His kingdom?

4. Read Mark 16:15. How have Jesus's words further motivated you to share God's love with people who have not experienced it?

5. What makes the unique stories of individuals who've experienced God's love and grace so compelling? How is your own story of being saved and transformed a sign of God's power, love, and grace?

6. Read Isaiah 6:1–8. From the story, we see that Isaiah was not the perfect man for the job of delivering God's message. Yet God used him anyway. What is holding you back from allowing God to use you to share His gospel with others?

CHAPTER 3

What's Your Motivation?

"I have but one passion: It is He, it is He alone.
The world is the field and the field is the world;
and henceforth that country shall be my home
where I can be most used in winning souls for Christ."

COUNT NICOLAUS LUDWIG VON ZINZENDORF

One afternoon, as I was greeting visitors outside the front entrance of our church campus in West Los Angeles, I spotted eight-division world champion boxer Manny Pacquiao. He was like the eye of a hurricane, standing calmly in the center of a throng of at least a hundred people. Whenever he moved, they moved.

Manny made his way over to me and said hello. Everybody gathered around. We shook hands, and I thanked him for coming.

"If there's anything I can do for you, or if there's anything you need, please let me know," I told him.

He replied, "I'd love to have you come speak at chapel at my house."

I soon learned that Manny, who is from the Philippines, trains at the Freddie Roach's Wild Card Boxing Club down in Hollywood whenever he's in town and stays at a house nearby. Oftentimes his mother can be seen sitting ringside during his fights, and his mother's sister—Manny's aunt—goes to our Westside campus and had invited him to church. Manny attends our church whenever he's training in Los Angeles.

I was honored and surprised by an invitation to preach at his home in Southern California.

I was also a bit nervous.

At the time I didn't know Manny very well. When I arrived at his house, the large entryway and living room were teeming with people. It was standing room only, and I didn't know *anyone*. I felt like everyone was staring at me because I was the only six-foot-five non-Filipino in the place.

To my relief, the attention quickly shifted to Manny. He entered the room, walked right through the crowd, and went to the front of the room.

He smiled and motioned to me, so I followed him and found a seat near where he stood. Then he picked up a microphone and faced the wall over in a corner by himself, with his back to the rest of the people. He began singing a worship song in a soft voice.

The crowd hushed.

At about the time Manny reached the chorus of the song, his worship team and everyone else joined him in singing. The entire scene was humbling. It was gentle. It was spiritual. It was very moving to see this man walk among his peers in a completely unpretentious manner and lead worship to Almighty God.

Manny sat down, and the praise team continued with a couple more songs. Then Manny stood up and introduced me as the pastor of his church. He told everyone that he had asked me to speak, and I shared a gospel message for about thirty minutes.

Afterward we went into another room to eat. There was one table with about six chairs, and Manny sat at the head of the table. I sat to his immediate right. A couple of other people sat down, but everyone else stood, talking with one another and eating plates of delicious, fragrant Filipino food. Manny and I talked as if we were the only two people in the room.

"How many of these people are your relatives?" I asked him.

He looked around the room and said, "None of them."

I said, "Well, there's your aunt. She's one."

"Oh," Manny replied. "She's the only one."

"So there's not another relative here?"

"No, these are all just friends."

"How did they all get in here?" I asked.

He said, "I invited them. Anyone is welcome."

"Do you feed them every night?"

Manny responded, "Well, Pastor, haven't you ever read your Bible?"

"Yes," I said with a smile, surprised by his humor.

"Every time Jesus taught, He always fed the people after," Manny began. "So after every chapel, we feed everybody. When I preached in the Philippines, thirty-four thousand people showed up, and I fed every one of them afterward."

"How often do you have this chapel?" I inquired. Manny must have felt like this was a game of Twenty Questions.

He said, "Every night."

"So you have all these people that are not your relatives—they're just Filipino people who show up here—and you have a Bible study and you feed them?"

He said, "Every night."

"Don't you feel like you need to get some rest or feel pressure because you've got a big fight coming up?"

"I ask everyone to leave at nine o'clock," he explained.

"Don't you need a little peace and quiet?"

"No, I feed on this," Manny said. "This is my life."

The Night Everything Changed

Serving Jesus and serving others was not always Manny Pacquiao's life. He has been very open about the way he used to live before he surrendered his life to the Lord.

On May 2, 2015, Manny Pacquiao fought Floyd Mayweather Jr. in a match that was billed as "The Fight of the Century." A couple of weeks before that much-anticipated fight, Manny allowed me to interview him at our church. Every seat in the theater was filled. Many people were not believers and came simply to see and hear from a boxing legend. In that interview he talked about how he grew up in abject poverty and began boxing at a very young age to earn money to help buy food for his mother and his siblings.

He won his first fight and was paid one hundred pesos, which is the equivalent of two dollars in the United States. Manny kept winning and eventually achieved great fame and wealth in his young life, but it had gone to his head. He shared during our interview that he gambled, drank, and womanized. He said,

At that time, I believed to myself that I know God, that I believe in God. I'm always praying every day—praying five times a day. After, I go drinking with my friends and gambling. . . . I thought I was a Christian, but I was just deceiving myself. My life before [was] always fighting with my wife. If you know the story of our family, we almost [broke] up. We don't talk to each other. Just her lawyer and my lawyer have conversations. There [were] a lot of problems, and even though we have a lot of money— it's empty. And that's how I found Jesus and decided to follow God.[1]

Manny revealed in his 2015 self-titled documentary that God spoke to him in a dream and said, "Son, why [did] you leave me? Why [did] you walk away from me?"[2] When the young boxer woke up, his pillow was soaking wet from his tears. He said that after this encounter with the Lord, he began reading his Bible with new eyes and was then transformed into a real servant and follower of Christ.

Though they were on the brink of divorce, Manny's wife, Jinkee, forgave him. She told her husband, "You have to leave all the worldly things. The gambling, being unfaithful. All of that. You have to change that. You are now a new creation of God, a new man, a changed man. So you better leave those things."

Manny owned a casino, and he sold it. He owned a bar, and he sold that too. He stopped drinking, partying with friends, and gambling. Manny is indeed a changed man, and he has a new motivation in life. Manny has discovered that to be driven by the love of Christ and the truth of His gospel is the best, most satisfying pursuit anyone could ever undertake.

Big Business

Scores of people today are motivated by the same things that once motivated Manny Pacquaio—fame, money, power, and pleasure. In fact, these motivations have become a $10 billion industry with folks eagerly handing over their time and money for self-help books, online courses, and motivational seminars.[3] We want to know the secret to becoming a one-minute manager and a million-aire next door. We want to enjoy a shorter workweek and to sculpt our bodies in ten days so we can master the art of attraction. We'll research, pore over countless quotes from historic figures, and analyze the habits of successful people in order to distill the truth of what truly compels us.

Your motivation is the reason why you do what you do. It's the thing, person, feeling, or goal that drives you to act. It's whatever you're living for.

To put it simply, we're either driven by eternal motivations or by worldly motivations. One example of a worldly motivation would be money or financial reward. Employees work hard for the promise of raises, incentives, and bonuses. Professional athletes work tirelessly for large contracts and signing bonuses. Sales teams rally together to achieve the best sales in their region and win their all-expenses paid trips to coastal destinations. Money is a powerful motivator, albeit a temporary one. After all, as Proverbs 23:5 says, "Cast but a glance at riches, and they are gone, for they will surely sprout wings and fly off to the sky like an eagle."

> Your motivation is the reason why you do what you do. It's the thing, person, feeling, or goal that drives you to act. It's whatever you're living for.

For some, money means nothing, but success and accomplishment are everything. Parents will make big financial sacrifices in order to prepare their child to become the next president, CEO, or neurosurgeon. A college student will practically live in the library in order to make the dean's list. Musicians may practice until their fingers are bloody for a standing ovation. Success feels good. Like the other motivations, it can be quite seductive—making us feel important, even "better than" others. Success leads us to believe we have done something worthwhile with our lives. But again, it is only a temporary motivator.

Another popular worldly motivation is the desire to affect change and influence. Every year millions of people from around the world give to causes larger than themselves, wanting to make a difference. Church mission outreaches to indigenous people groups; marathons for medical research, disaster relief teams, the Peace Corps, the Red Cross, and many more organizations draw volunteers from all walks of life, all of them hoping to show that their lives mean something.

The desire to make a positive change on this planet is a good thing, and there are many important causes to rally behind. But if that becomes our main focus, or we seek to obtain meaning and significance in our charitable work, we miss an incomparable opportunity to make a spiritual and an eternal difference in the lives of others.

It's No Secret

Temporary motivations distract mankind from the truth. Even as Christians we may fool ourselves into believing that making money or being liked is more important the preaching the gospel. Success, notoriety, and influence can call to us like sirens, pulling us into their unfulfilling whirlpools. Clever deception masquerades as authenticity, and temptation abounds.

We live in a day and age when sound doctrine is being replaced with self-serving ideas that are devoid of spiritual truth. Churches across the world are dying because they no longer accurately preach and teach God's Word. It is quite possible that we have arrived at the dreadful hour Paul warned his disciple Timothy about. A time "when people will not put up with sound doctrine. Instead, to suit their own desires, they will gather around them a great number of teachers to say what their itching ears want to hear" (2 Timothy 4:3).

Paul also predicted that there would be terrible times in the last days. In 2 Timothy 3:2–5, he wrote,

> People will be lovers of themselves, lovers of money, boastful, proud, abusive, disobedient to their parents, ungrateful, unholy, without love, unforgiving, slanderous, without self-control, brutal, not lovers of the good, treacherous, rash, conceited, lovers of pleasure rather than lovers of God—having a form of godliness but denying its power.

Does any of this sound familiar to you? To love oneself is humanism. To love money is materialism. To love pleasure is hedonism. All three are major motivators in the world today.

Since its release in 2006, a self-help book titled *The Secret* has sold more than nineteen million copies worldwide and has been translated into over forty-six languages. The premise of the book is that you can create whatever you want by using the power of your mind. It is a self-centered philosophy that is actually nothing more than recycled Hinduism and New Age folly. Many people think if Oprah endorses something, that makes it okay.

According to the book, to attract your perfect weight you just think it in your mind and then you become it![4] (Oh, if that only were true—I would have six-pack abs and a full head of hair!) The book also suggests that everyone has his or her own personal genie standing by with a "your wish is my command" policy. I want to share with you what one fan of *The Secret* wrote—not to poke fun, but to demonstrate how far the world has come in creating substitutions for a relationship with Christ:

The one thing that stuck with me was the Genie. I immediately felt a connection to this concept.

I drew a Genie with a handsome face, a look of satisfaction and a perfect body to compliment it.

He is there in my room on the wall and he is like the most perfect thing that ever happened to me! Be it exams, practicals, relationship problems, health problems, or just something I am scared of, I just tell it to Genie and believe that he will manage it somehow.

After telling my problem to Genie and asking him to take care [of] it, I just stop thinking about it. Somewhere in my heart I feel that he'll take care of it, and trust me, he has never failed me once!

He is my universe, my personal Genie and he fulfills all my wishes, no limitations.[5]

When I read this testimonial, I can't help but feel both sadness and frustration that such a simple book could lead so many people astray. Jesus Christ—not an imaginary genie—is real and alive (Ephesians 1:19–20). He is the One who truly cares and asks us to cast all our burdens upon Him (1 Peter 5:7). Hebrews 1:3 puts it this way:

The Son is the radiance of God's glory and the exact representation of his being, sustaining all things by his powerful word. After he had provided purification for sins, he sat down at the right hand of the Majesty in heaven.

In its futile attempt to be the answer for all of mankind's needs, *The Secret* fails to address the most basic reality of life: death!

If the Law of Attraction really worked, then no one would ever die, because most people would like to live forever. This fact became painfully clear when a viewer of the *Oprah* show, after seeing two episodes dedicated to *The Secret*, wrote to Oprah to "announce that she had decided to halt her breast-cancer treatments and heal herself with her mind."[6]

True Motivation

The truth is, God offers eternity through Jesus Christ alone (John 3:16). His living words are the only words of eternal life (see John 6:68 and Hebrews 4:12).

All other religions began with people asking, "How can we get to God?" That's a very good question. And in the attempt to find an answer, many different people came up with their own moral systems. They said in essence, "Let's do these things to get to God. And if we do enough of these good things, we'll get to heaven." (Or, in New Age thinking, "find peace within ourselves.")

In Christianity, *God* looks down from heaven and wants to redeem mankind. So He left heaven and came to this earth in the form of a baby to bring salvation to the earth. His name was Jesus. He lived thirty-three years and never committed a sin. Then He died on a cross as atonement for our sins so we could have eternal life. No other man in the history of the world—and certainly not a make-believe genie—has ever done such a thing for humanity.

There is no other substitute for Jesus's love. Every other attempt falls devastatingly short because it will have zero ability to change our hearts, cure our sin, or impact our eternal destiny. Christ's love is our true motivation, and it propels us toward greater feats than we ever thought possible. We will share His truth with the world so that as many people as possible can have a relationship with God and spend eternity with Him in heaven. That's what being compelled to tell is all about! It's a passion that will get us out of bed in the morning better than any alarm clock, deadline, or sales goal. It'll help us endure pain, sorrow, and hardship in order to tell others about the best thing that has ever happened to us.

"This Is My Plan!"

During his life, Manny Pacquiao has seen that all the wealth and fame and pleasure in the world ultimately add up to nothing. Now he chooses to use his platform, influence, time, and energy to point to and invest in that which is eternal.

During my interview with Manny, I said to him, "There are people who are chasing the very things you were chasing, and they believe these things bring happiness. You had this conversion experience where God completely transformed you. What would you say to someone here today who's living in the world? Having been there, what would you say to encourage them to give their life to the Lord and to let go of those things?"

Manny answered, "All I can say to them is you better know Jesus—have Jesus in your life—because without Jesus in your life, your life is not complete. Only Jesus can complete your everything. Me and my wife, we understand it's because we have Jesus. We have the love of God every day. Not money. Nothing can compare to our happiness right now."

> Christ's love is our true motivation, and it propels us toward greater feats than we ever thought possible.

About six months before the big match between him and Mayweather, Manny asked me to speak at his chapel service the night before his fight against Chris Algieri in Macau, China. I agreed, and when I arrived at the hotel in Macau, there were all these people gathered around from his team. Manny pulled me off to the side and said, "Pastor, this is my plan."

I said, "What's that?"

He replied, "To get all these people here and have you tell them about Jesus."

Manny understands why we're here—that our main mission as believers is to tell others about Christ. The risen Lord is the only cure for what's ailing this world. He is the only One who can fill the empty space in our hearts. In a world filled with counterfeits and substitutions, people need to know:

> Salvation is found in no one else, for there is no other name under heaven given to mankind by which we must be saved. (Acts 4:12)

You and I know firsthand what it's like to have held the wrong motivations in life, because we were rescued from them on the day we were saved. I don't know your story personally, but my guess is that you may have pursued false religions and New Age theories, entertainment and celebrities, sex and ungodly relationships, health and wealth, work, or selfish gain before you gave your life to the Lord. You now have a new cause in Christ. You can tell people where you've been and how God delivered you. You can declare, as David did in Psalm 40:2:

> He lifted me out of the slimy pit,
>   out of the mud and mire;
> he set my feet on a rock
>   and gave me a firm place to stand.

Each day before you get out of bed in the morning—before your feet even touch the floor—pray and thank God for saving you and for all His blessings. Then say, "God, use me today. Show me how I can be a vessel for You and Your kingdom today. You are my portion, my life, and my motivation." If you start each day with this sincere prayer, it will serve as a powerful reminder of what drives and compels you, and I guarantee that God will open your eyes to new opportunities to be a light for Him and to make an impact for eternity.

DISCUSSION QUESTIONS

1. What were the motivations you used to have in life before meeting Jesus? Do you struggle with those same motivations today? What does 1 Peter 4:1–7 teach us about these desires and what God would have us do?

2. Like Manny Pacquiao, how are you using the opportunity of the relationships God has given you to share His Word with them?

3. Read 2 Timothy 3:2–5. How do these words illustrate the many negative motivations that drive people today? What other negative motivations do you see in our culture?

4. Read Ecclesiastes 7:27–29. What do these verses teach us about how God created man? What do we learn about mankind's tendency? Now read Ecclesiastes 12:13–14. After experiencing all life had to offer and writing the entire book of Ecclesiastes to share his wisdom, what did King Solomon conclude?

5. In your own words after reading the section "True Motivation" on page 48, how would you explain to someone the differences between Christianity and other religions?

CHAPTER 4

Embracing Eternity

"We shall have all eternity to celebrate our victories,
but we have only one swift hour
before the sunset in which to win them."

ROBERT MOFFAT

In the year 2000, Australia, "the Land Down Under," took the world stage for two special events: the welcoming of a brand-new millennium and the summer Olympic Games.

As the clock struck midnight on January 1, 2000, a barrage of fireworks exploded from the Sydney Harbor Bridge, lighting up the entire port. Over one million people gathered to watch the New Year's celebration, while millions more watched it on television—some also intently watching their computers to see if the Y2K bug was indeed fact or fiction.

Later that summer, Sydney hosted the Olympic Games. Once again, the Harbor Bridge was the central focus as billions of people watched the televised opening ceremonies.

These two events shared a lot of things in common: the same city, same landmark, a huge fireworks display, and the attention of the entire world. However, they shared another similarity, which—at the moment—probably didn't make much sense.

At the end of the New Year's Eve celebration, the Harbor Bridge was not lit with the year *2000*, nor did the Olympic opening ceremonies conclude with a fiery display of the five Olympic rings. In each case, the Harbor Bridge was illuminated by the same word:

Eternity

Many people had to have been scratching their heads and asking themselves, "What does eternity have to do with New Year's Eve or the Olympics?" Honestly, not much! But, as random as it might have seemed, this word is a meaningful part of Sydney's history. It's a reference to Arthur Stace, a.k.a. the "graffiti preacher."

Arthur Stace was born and raised in Australia, in a home where alcoholism, hopelessness, and poverty were part of his everyday life. At the age of twelve and with no formal education, he became a ward of the state. By age fifteen, he was sent to jail for the first time. In his twenties, Arthur became a recruiter for his sister's brothels, and most of his early adult life was spent as a miserable petty thief and an alcoholic.

Until August 6, 1930.

That was the day forty-six-year-old Arthur Stace put his faith in Jesus Christ, and his life was never the same. Two years later, Arthur Stace was in church and heard an evangelist named John Ridley preach a message entitled "The Echoes of Eternity." His Bible passage was from Isaiah 57:15:

> For thus saith the high and lofty One that inhabiteth eternity, whose name is Holy; I dwell in the high and holy

place, with him also that is of a contrite and humble spirit,
to revive the spirit of the humble, and to revive the heart
of the contrite ones. (KJV)

This beautiful verse begins by revealing that God towers above us and inhabits eternity! John Ridley was so moved by these words that he said, "Eternity, eternity, I wish that I could sound or shout that word to everyone in the streets of Sydney. You've got to meet it. Where will you spend eternity?"[1]

Those words were all Arthur Stace needed to launch his now famous evangelism campaign.

For the next thirty-five years, Arthur, who was basically illiterate and could not even write his own name, began a simple routine. Every morning he would wake up at 4:00 a.m. and spend an hour in prayer. Around 5:00 a.m., he would leave his house and go wherever he felt God was leading him. For hours, he would take a piece of chalk and write one word—*Eternity*—in beautiful script wherever he could. Every one hundred feet, Arthur wrote his one-word sermon throughout the sidewalks in Sydney. As his efforts continued, he somehow avoided being arrested on more than twenty occasions for defacing public property, always answering questions with, "I have permission from a higher source."

For more than twenty years, his work remained a mystery. It caused multitudes of people to pause and ponder. The power of that one word was felt throughout the entire city. Eventually an entire nation was touched.

Finally, in 1956, the mystery was solved as Arthur Stace was revealed as the "graffiti preacher." Hordes of people he never knew personally thanked him for the impact he had on their lives. Arthur Stace died in 1967, but his message was secured for generations to come:

- The bell in the Sydney GPO clock tower, rebuilt in 1960, bears the word *Eternity*.
- *Eternity* is inscribed on a copper plate in the middle of Sydney's town hall square.
- In 2000, the Sydney Harbor Bridge shouted his message for the entire world to see . . . twice!
- In 2003, the opera *The Eternity Man* was written based on Stace's life story.
- In 2008, *The Eternity Man* was adapted into film.

Arthur Stace's remarkable story demonstrates the impact one person, willing to be used by God, can have on others—even an entire nation—for Jesus Christ. I'm reminded of the quote from the movie *Gladiator*, where Maximus Decimus Meridius declares to his men in a passionate speech, "Brothers, what we do in life echoes in eternity." No doubt, Mr. Stace's simple mission had ripple effects of eternal proportions.

Woven into the Gospel

Can you imagine if there was an Arthur Stace in every corner of the world? What if just one believer in every city was motivated by an immense burden and a daily mission to bring ETERNITY to the forefront of everyone's attention?

These questions consumed my thoughts when I attended the Olympic Games in China in 2008. Not the fanfare or the excitement . . . not the gold medals or records broken . . . but the droves of people wandering around Beijing who did not know the name of Jesus.

The summer and winter Olympics display the incredible physical skill and strength of the best athletes on the planet. Of course they are thrilling moments in time. But when they conclude after seventeen days every four years, they end up being just that—mere moments in time when compared to the infinite span of eternity.

There is a greater test of strength and endurance happening right now. There is a superior crown to be obtained. Paul described it this way in Philippians 3:12–14:

> Not that I have already obtained all this, or have already arrived at my goal, but I press on to take hold of that for which Christ Jesus took hold of me. Brothers and sisters, I do not consider myself yet to have taken hold of it. But one thing I do: Forgetting what is behind and straining toward what is ahead, I press on toward the goal to win the prize for which God has called me heavenward in Christ Jesus.

No goal in this life is as important as our heavenly calling: to spend eternity with our Lord and to invite as many people as possible to the same glorious future. As C. S. Lewis wrote, "All that is not eternal is eternally useless."

Eternity is woven into the gospel! One of the very first scriptures anyone commits to memory as a child is John 3:16, in which Jesus promised eternity with Him in heaven: "For God so loved the world that He gave His only begotten Son, that whoever believes in him should not perish but have everlasting life."

The apostle Paul echoed this truth by writing in Romans 6:23 that "the gift of God is eternal life in Christ Jesus our Lord." Every time you see a rainbow, it's a vivid reminder of God's "everlasting covenant" never to destroy the earth again by water.[2] Psalm 100:5 declares that God's

> No goal in this life is as important as our heavenly calling: to spend eternity with our Lord and to invite as many people as possible to the same glorious future.

"mercy is everlasting" (NKJV). His throne has been established from "everlasting to everlasting."[3] He is the "King eternal,"[4] the "Alpha and Omega—the beginning and the end,"[5] who has established an "eternal purpose" for all mankind.[6]

How can our finite minds grasp what is infinite? We often exaggerate a lengthy situation or process by declaring, "That seemed like an eternity!" But we really don't understand the full scope of eternity.

Imagine a bird disassembling the earth—twig by twig, leaf by leaf, pebble by pebble—and taking every individual element to the moon, piece by piece. When this task was finally completed, eternity would just be starting! If every five hundred years, a hummingbird sharpened his beak on granite rock that stood five hundred miles high and five hundred miles wide, once the rock was completely eroded, it would be but one second of eternity!

When we begin to grasp what eternity really means, and realize that everybody on this planet will one day come face-to-face with their eternal destiny, it raises the stakes. It compels us not only to care but also to speak. No longer can we keep quiet! Our words and thoughts must be intentional. How could we *not* share the gospel with our friends? How could we stand by and say nothing, knowing our loved ones could spend an eternity separated from God?

When we consider the "eternalness" of eternity, we have no choice . . . we must share Jesus!

Ticking Clock

Every single day, no matter where you go, you are surrounded by people who do not have a saving knowledge of the truth. At work or at school, at the gym or at the mall. At restaurants, grocery stores, coffee shops, and movie theaters. Maybe even in your own home. You encounter people who have never had the gospel explained to them. They might know something *about* God, but simply knowing about God doesn't change a person's soul. In fact, the Bible says that when people are following the ways of the world, they are dead in their sins (Ephesians 2:1–3).

This is critically important because every twenty-four hours, approximately 150,000 people die and face their Creator. Every hour, 6,316 people take their last breath. Every minute, 105 people are ushered into eternity.[7]

When I first moved to California, I had been living in the San Fernando Valley for only a couple of weeks before witnessing a horrible car accident. I was traveling south on Balboa Boulevard, about to turn right on Rinaldi Street toward Hillcrest Christian Church where I pastored. A car ahead of me, traveling in the same direction as I had been, somehow veered into the northbound traffic and crashed head-on into an eighteen-wheeler. There were no bystanders, so I pulled over and ran to the vehicle. When I looked inside the window, there was a lady there in the front seat, but there was no life in her. She was beyond resuscitation. Her spirit had left the earthly vessel we call a body, and she was gone.

I felt immense sadness in that moment. I didn't know who she was, but I was certain she had a family who loved her, who would grieve and miss her terribly. As I drove away that morning, I couldn't help but wonder about this woman's eternal destiny. I hoped she knew Jesus. I wished that I had had a chance to tell her about Him, but she was gone. One minute she was here, and the next minute she was in eternity.

My friend, the clock never stops. Time does not stand still for anyone. People are continually exiting this life—many without any hope. Hebrews 9:27–28 (NKJV) says,

And as it is appointed for men to die once, but after this the judgment, so Christ was offered once to bear the sins of many.

How many precious souls do you know personally who will stand before God on Judgment Day without Jesus by their side to advocate for them, rescuing them from an eternity separated from God's love, light, and peace?

Eternal Reality

I'm going to take a risk here by wading into an unpopular and uncomfortable topic early on in this book. I promise you that our journey together will be challenging, joyful, inspiring, and maybe even exciting at times. But there is also a hard truth that can't be ignored, and it is this:

Everyone is going to spend an eternity somewhere.

Your coworkers, your friends, and your family members will all, one day, step into eternity. What do they believe? While many people have adopted the philosophy that there are numerous ways to obtain salvation, Christ our Lord set the record straight:

Jesus answered, "I am the way and the truth and the life. No one comes to the Father except through me." (John 14:6)

Think about that truth for a moment: no one is going to get into heaven unless they have a personal relationship with God's one and only Son, the Lord Jesus Christ. And anyone who is not in Christ will be lost. We learn from the Scripture that there is an eternal reality that awaits those who reject the truth of salvation. It is called hell.

I would be remiss not to delve into this subject in a book about sharing our faith. How could I talk about salvation—which is "the act of saving or protecting from harm, risk, loss, destruction"—without mentioning what it is we are being saved *from*?

We are being saved from the ultimate consequence of sin: hell. In Mark 9:47–49, Christ quoted the prophet Isaiah when He described hell as a place where "their worm does not die and the fire is not quenched" (NKJV). Seven times in the Bible, Jesus said hell is a place where "there will be weeping and gnashing of teeth."[8] Peter declared, "By the same word the present heavens and earth are reserved for fire, being kept for the day of judgment and destruction of the ungodly" (2 Peter 3:7).

We learn from Jesus's parable of the rich man and Lazarus that "a great chasm has been set in place" between heaven and hades so that no one can cross over (Luke 16:26). And the apostle John boldly stated in Revelation 20:15 that if anyone's name is not found written in the Book of Life, he will be thrown into "the lake of fire."

Despite how frequently and clearly the Bible discusses hell, many people today deny or ignore its existence. There are even pastors and authors who have constructed their own theology about God's judgment, conveniently omitting or reinterpreting numerous scriptures about eternal separation from God and inventing an unjust god who turns a blind eye to evil.

In Jude, one of the shortest books in the Bible, we find a crucial reminder about our mission to save people from the flames of hell. In fact, Jude, a servant of Jesus Christ and a brother of James, "felt *compelled* to write" this even though he had hoped to instead write to them about salvation (v. 3). The matter was so serious, he had to address it:

> Though you already know all this, I want to remind you that the Lord at one time delivered his people out of Egypt, but later destroyed those who did not believe. And

the angels who did not keep their positions of authority but abandoned their proper dwelling—these he has kept in darkness, bound with everlasting chains for judgment on the great Day. In a similar way, Sodom and Gomorrah and the surrounding towns gave themselves up to sexual immorality and perversion. They serve as an example of those who suffer the punishment of eternal fire. (vv. 5–7)

These are difficult words to read. I realize that it would be much more pleasant to talk about heaven (which we will do shortly) than the topic of hell. But I must adopt the same attitude as Paul who "did not shrink from declaring to you the whole counsel of God" (Acts 20:27 ESV).

We have to talk about the good, the bad, and the ugly regarding the spiritual decisions we make as human beings—and the consequences of those decisions. Understanding the reality of hell is one reason why we will find ourselves compelled to tell our friends and neighbors about the good news of Jesus Christ. To be eternally separated from the presence and goodness of God is an unimaginable thing.

Rescued from the Flames

When I was just out of Bible college, there was a single mother who attended the small church where I was preaching. On one particularly cold and snowy Sunday afternoon, she returned home after church and put on a long nightgown over her clothes for some extra warmth. As she walked through her house, her nightgown grazed against a small foot furnace. Within moments, she was completely engulfed in flames. Even though she managed to extinguish the fire, she was left with second- and third-degree burns over 70 percent of her body. She was rushed to the hospital's burn center for treatment and care.

When I went to visit her, I had no idea what awaited me. It was my first visit to a burn center. I knew she would be in bad shape, but to what extent I did not know. When I entered the facility, what I saw became forever etched into my mind. Patients were screaming and moaning from their pain and anguish. The stench of burnt flesh permeated every hallway. Everyday people had their lives completely turned upside down because of one accident.

> Salvation through faith in Christ is more than spiritual "fire insurance." It is the "blessed assurance" of living eternally with God!

Without a doubt, this was, and still remains, one of the most horrific experiences I have ever encountered. But something more horrifying and real about that day remains with me: that it was just a glimpse, a snapshot, of what hell is like.

Salvation through faith in Christ is more than spiritual "fire insurance." It is the "blessed assurance" of living eternally with God! When you share your faith with someone, you are grabbing hold of a once-in-a-lifetime opportunity to lead that person away from the flames and into the unmatched goodness, security, and peace of an everlasting Father who loves them. Yes, sometimes you will get multiple opportunities to plant seeds of faith or to water those seeds, but you never know what time will allow. So, since time is of the essence, let's make every opportunity count.

> Be very careful, then, how you live—not as unwise but as wise, making the most of every opportunity, because the days are evil. (Ephesians 5:15–16)

For a Limited Time Only

While eternity spans across an infinite continuum, time on earth is limited. We don't have all the time in the world to tell everyone we know about the good news. We must have a sense of urgency to share the gospel because Jesus is either coming back in our lifetime or our lives will eventually end. Either way, we will at some point run out of opportunities to share the gospel—and others will run out of time to put their faith in Jesus.

He is our one and only hope.

Probably one of the most impressive displays of this hope was a greeting that was used by the early church. First-century Christians would greet each other with a peculiar word that produced a spiritual hope every time it was spoken.

The greeting was, "Maranatha!"

Not "hello," not "good-bye," but "Maranatha!" Even though this greeting is very uncommon today, *Maranatha* is a word of weighty significance. It literally means "the Lord is coming soon" in Aramaic. Talk about a great way to start and end a conversation! Imagine the great expectation of Christ's return the early Christians must have had. What comfort they received just knowing that one day Jesus would return to the earth. They kept it on the forefront of their minds and in their daily conversations. Actually, they were only echoing what Jesus said,

> Look, I am coming soon! My reward is with me, and I will give to each person according to what they have done. (Revelation 22:12)

Fast-forward two thousand years. Just think how it would change our daily actions if we were this cognizant of the return of Christ? What if every Christian, worldwide, started and ended their conversations with, "Hey, Jesus is coming soon"? It would undoubtedly change our outlook and response to every person we encountered. But *Maranatha* is much more than a greeting, a welcome, or an encouraging word.

It is, in fact, a reality.

Jesus *is* returning to this earth—soon!

The Bible clearly says that one day the Lord will come down from heaven, with the voice of the archangel, and Jesus will take those who are ready away from this earth.[9] What an awesome day that will be! To see Jesus face-to-face and live in heaven with Him for eternity is the ultimate reward for every believer. Jesus Himself said in Matthew 24:42:

Therefore keep watch, because you do not know on what day your Lord will come.

This long-awaited, amazing, glorious day will happen! And when Jesus returns, He will hold every one of us accountable for how we managed and used the resources, abilities, opportunities, and the good news He placed into our hands.

For those of us who know and love Jesus, this is not something to fear. It is something to be excited about! It should spark in us a sense of urgency that until that day comes, we have an important job to do. We must tell everyone we meet about the gospel of Jesus Christ.

If you knew Jesus was coming back next week, whom would you tell about Him today? Think about your list of five names you made at the start of this book. Now take a deep breath, close your eyes, and ask God to give you the courage to do what I'm about to ask you to do next: pick up your phone right now and call or send a text message to the people on your list and invite them individually to come to your church or Bible study this week. (Keep in mind: a phone call will be the warmest and most personal method—and perhaps the hardest to refuse.)

I'll wait . . .

If you're tempted to skip this activity and continue reading, I have to ask: If not today, then when? Now is the time, my friend!

Okay, now that your invitation has been sent out, there's no turning back. Do you feel a sense of relief or excitement? You should! You're about to share with someone the most important thing in your life—Jesus!

Since none of us knows when Jesus will come back or how much time we have left on this earth, let's make each day count. We are standing on the edge of eternity and have a profound opportunity to invite the people in our life to step into a relationship with God today and a forever spent with Him in heaven.

Head in the Clouds

Have you ever been told that you've got your head in the clouds? It's an expression that means you've been daydreaming, not paying attention, or maintaining unrealistic ideas. Paul encouraged us in Colossians 3:1 that since we've been raised with Christ our Lord, we ought to seek things that are from above, because that is where Christ is seated at the right hand of God. Then he wrote in verses 2 and 3,

> Set your mind on things above, not on things on the earth. For you died, and your life is hidden with Christ in God. (NKJV)

Paul was saying that as a Christian, you ought to have your head in the clouds in a different way. You should be looking up toward heaven—toward eternal matters. Yes, there are earthly matters we cannot ignore, such as bills to pay, our family to take care of, work, education, etc. But we should not become overly preoccupied with them. We must concern ourselves primarily with things of eternal importance, such as our spiritual development, meeting the needs of the poor, sharing the gospel, and discipling others.

In 1 Peter 2:11, Peter wrote that we are "foreigners and exiles [and] to abstain from sinful desires, which wage war against your soul." In other words, you and I are aliens in the world, so we should not get too comfortable here! We should not do the things that people in the world do, because we come from a different culture, a heavenly one. One day you and I and everyone who has put their faith in Jesus Christ will spend an eternity in heaven. We don't have time to cling to anything worldly because we are just passing through. First John 2:15–17 puts it this way:

Do not love the world or anything in the world. If anyone loves the world, love for the Father is not in them. For everything in the world—the lust of the flesh, the lust of the eyes, and the pride of life—comes not from the Father but from the world. The world and its desires pass away, but whoever does the will of God lives forever.

Setting our hearts and minds on eternity also helps us maintain a proper perspective when faced with issues that right now may seem too difficult. When we consider eternity's length, we realize that our troubles are "light and momentary," as 2 Corinthians

4:17 explains, and "are achieving for us an eternal glory that far outweighs them all."

Heavenly Home

After everything we've endured, after we've run a good race on this earth, believers in Jesus Christ are promised an eternity in heaven.

Heaven is not a figment of someone's imagination or a mystical fairy tale. It is just as real as the world you and I live in right now.

Can you imagine this glorious city? Are you thinking of fluffy clouds? Angels strumming harps? Philadelphia Cream Cheese? No, no, no. Forget about what you've seen in commercials, movies, and cartoons. Let's look to the Bible for the truth about heaven. In Revelation 21:18–21, John used the most precious elements known to man to describe the very foundations of this majestic metropolis:

> The wall was made of jasper, and the city of pure gold, as pure as glass. The foundations of the city walls were decorated with every kind of precious stone. The first foundation was jasper, the second sapphire, the third agate, the fourth emerald, the fifth onyx, the sixth ruby, the seventh chrysolite, the eighth beryl, the ninth topaz, the tenth turquoise, the eleventh jacinth, and the twelfth amethyst. The twelve gates were twelve pearls, each gate made of a single pearl. The great street of the city was of gold, as pure as transparent glass.

Here on earth, we would never dream of walking on gold! Gold so pure that it's like *transparent glass*, no less! But the God of the universe reserved the choicest materials to build a heavenly city for those who love Him, so even the material upon which our feet would walk would be made from the same stuff that we scrimp and save and sock away for just to have a morsel of it in a small ring or a delicate necklace. Nothing this world has to offer—not even the best things here on earth—can ever satisfy us or come close to what God intended for us at creation, which will one day be restored when Jesus returns and we go to be with Him in heaven.

Just before Jesus was betrayed, He comforted His disciples with these words:

> Do not let your hearts be troubled. You believe in God; believe also in me. My Father's house has many rooms; if that were not so, would I have told you that I am going there to prepare a place for you? (John 14:1–2)

What a mind-blowing promise for everyone who believes in Jesus Christ! This very moment Jesus is in the heavenly realm laying foundations, framing walls, tiling floors, hanging pictures, building cabinets, and planting gardens . . . just for us. Here's the thing I can't comprehend: Jesus loves us so much that He humbled Himself as a man and died for our sins more than two thousand years ago. *The work He did on the cross was more than enough.* And yet He continues to love, give, and provide for us. He continues to work on our behalf by preparing our heavenly home. How astounding is the love of Christ!

Trustworthy and True

Heaven is our home. This earth, with all its troubles and tragedies, is not our permanent dwelling. Revelation 21:3 tells us that in heaven, God will be with us. He will make His dwelling among us, just as He walked in the Garden of Eden with Adam and Eve (Genesis 3:8–9). Verses 4 and 5 of Revelation 21 go on to reveal:

"He will wipe every tear from their eyes. There will be no more death or mourning or crying or pain, for the old order of things has passed away." He who was seated on the throne said, "I am making everything new!" Then he said, "Write this down, for these words are trustworthy and true."

These are words we can trust in: that in heaven there will be no more sorrow, disease, pain, crime, or death because Almighty God will make all things new. Oh, I can't wait for that day! How about you?

Heaven is that place we long for. It is where our friends and family who believed in the Lord and have passed are right now. It is the blessed hope that drives us to share the gospel. After all, what is the best way to invest in heaven? Isn't the best investment in the people with whom we share the good news? I don't know about you, but when I get there, I want it to be *filled* with people. I want to get there and see billions of people there, from every tribe and from every nation, all together worshiping the Lord in our heavenly home.

The only way that will happen is if you and I are compelled to tell the present world about our wonderful Savior and the truth of His gospel. Maybe you're fully on board with this truth, but you're still afraid. Let's remedy that fear in the next chapter.

DISCUSSION QUESTIONS

1. How does the reality of eternity change your daily life? Why does God embed the idea of eternity all throughout the Bible?

2. What excites you about eternity with Jesus? What scares you about eternity? What about the concept of eternity do you have difficulty describing?

3. According to Colossians 3:1–3, what should we set our minds upon and why?

4. Knowing that you only have a limited time on this earth, how should you change the manner in which you share Jesus with other people?

5. Read Philippians 3:12–14. What do we need to leave behind in order to strive forward toward eternity with God?

CHAPTER 5

The Value
of One Soul

"Is anything worth more than a soul?
The answer, obviously, is no.
God values the human soul. And so should we."

GREG LAURIE[1]

W hen I was young, my family and I would often drive over to a local lake in Kansas called Courtney Davis Lake Resort to spend the day. It was a picturesque setting with picnic benches nestled among lofty trees and songful birds flying overhead. There were large swings, diving platforms, and wooden rafts throughout the lake.

Sometimes we would head over with just our family. Other times we went with another family or a large group from church. My four siblings and I loved to run around and play, especially near the water.

One such idyllic afternoon took a frightening turn when someone ran over to my dad and shouted, "Debbie fell into the lake!"

Debbie is my older sister. She was six or seven years old at the time. Having been an animal lover from day one, it was no surprise that Debbie had become fascinated by little frogs that were swimming in the lake. Somehow she slipped and fell into the water.

No matter how hard she tried, there was no way she could get out because a sloped cement embankment surrounded the mass of water. And that embankment was covered in slippery moss.

She yelled to her friend Danny, who had been standing over her, paralyzed by fear, "Go get my dad!"

Meanwhile, I was in the picnic area, and I remember seeing Dad there with a full plate of food. He had just finished loading up his plate and he was about to sit down to eat. But when Danny ran toward us and announced what had happened to Debbie, my dad did not take the time to set his plate down on the picnic table. He immediately started running and just let the food fall to the ground.

My sister sent Danny to get our dad because she knew Dad would save her. As she groped at the slick embankment, she saw a group of people running across the grass toward her, with Dad racing way ahead of the pack. He swooped down, grabbed Debbie's arm, and plucked her out of the water.

She was covered in slimy moss, but none of us cared. We were all so grateful that Debbie had been rescued. Everyone cried tears of joy.

Looking back, Debbie says it seemed like Dad rescued her in an instant. Though he had been enjoying conversation and was about to eat his lunch, he dropped everything in the blink of an eye and sprinted to the lake—to save his daughter.

She was without hope until he arrived.

Why did my dad save my sister? I know that may seem like

a silly question. Any loving father would gladly save his own child from peril. And yet the rest of us were either frozen in fear or not nearly as fast as Dad was in getting to Debbie in time.

So let's dig deeper to understand the reasoning and psychology behind my dad's act of heroism. The answer is so critical to the topic of actually getting out there and sharing your faith. My dad saved my sister because of two compelling reasons:

1. **He knew *who* was lost.** His daughter. The little girl his wife carried in her womb for nine months. A child to whom they had read countless bedtime stories. They taught her how to walk and talk. They changed diapers (and this was back in the day before the disposable kind!) and potty trained her. They took care of her when she was sick. She was the only Deborah Rutherford in the world with her exact DNA. She was a precious, irreplaceable child.

2. **He knew *what it meant to be* lost.** Dad understood that if he didn't act quickly, his treasured daughter could drown. She would be gone forever. There would be no bringing her back. He had heard about enough of these tragic accidents happening in families to know the danger was real and imminent.

My dad understood the value of my sister's life, and he understood the implications of doing nothing about that desperate situation. He couldn't remain frozen in fear of loss or failure. My dad knew he had to act, and because of his courage—and the grace of God, of course—my sister is alive today.

The Great Paralyzer

Fear is the biggest reason why we don't get up from our comfy picnic bench and tell others about Jesus. Maybe you envision something going horribly wrong once you speak up about what you believe. Perhaps you're afraid you'll fail. Or look foolish. Or do more harm than good.

It's true that any time we choose to share Jesus with others we risk being rejected. However, we cannot let fear rule over us because it will stand in the way of the work God has called us to do. His plan and purpose often reach far beyond what we can see.

Throughout the Bible, we can find multiple instances where fear tripped up God's people:

> We cannot let fear rule over us because it will stand in the way of the work God has called us to do. His plan and purpose often reach far beyond what we can see.

- Adam was afraid because he sinned in the Garden so he hid himself from God (Genesis 3:10).
- Sarah laughed in disbelief at the Lord's promise, and when she was questioned about it, she lied because she was afraid (Genesis 18:15).
- Lot was afraid to stay in Zoar after the destruction of Sodom and Gomorrah so he and his daughters lived in a cave. Fear led to isolation, and isolation led Lot's daughter to devise the sinful scheme to get their father drunk and get pregnant by him (Genesis 19:30–38).
- In Genesis 26:6–8, when Isaac and his beautiful wife, Rebecca, lived in Gerar, Isaac lied and said that Rebecca was his sister because he was afraid that the men of that town would kill him in order to have her.

- Jacob, fearing his father-in-law, Laban, deceived Laban and fled from his home with his wives, Leah and Rachel. Laban pursued Jacob and may have harmed him had God not intervened (Genesis 31:22–32).

These are just some examples of fear in the book of Genesis! We could list many more instances of fear leading to many problems for God's people in Genesis and the other sixty-five books of the Bible, but that would probably fill an entire chapter or two on its own. I'd like to highlight one other example from Numbers 13, because fear caused an entire generation of people to miss out on the blessing of the Lord. I believe this biblical account relates so much to our need to be obedient to the call of sharing of faith.

Just to recap: The Israelites had been slaves in Egypt for four hundred years. God, through Moses, led His people out of bondage, and they forged ahead to the promised land. Moses wisely wanted to explore the land to know the danger they faced, so he sent twelve spies to scout out the land and report back what they discovered.

When the spies returned, they brought conflicting reports. Two of them, Caleb and Joshua, were adamant that the Israelites should march into Canaan with force and take the land for their possession. It was flowing with milk and honey, they said, and it was ripe for the taking.

However, the other ten spies disagreed. They were terrified by what they had seen. "We can't attack those people; they are stronger than we are," they said. "All the people we saw there are of great size. . . . We seemed like grasshoppers in our own eyes, and we looked the same to them" (vv. 31–33).

The people of Israel listened to the terrified ten instead of the tenacious two and refused to enter the land. Doubting and complaining, they turned away from what God had commanded them to do, so the Lord required them to wander in the wilderness until the next generation had replaced them (Numbers 14:20–35).

What was it that prevented them from entering the promised land?

Fear. Plain and simple.

They were afraid of the Canaanites, of their size and strength. And they refused to trust in the power of the Lord to see them through. The Israelites forgot about the One who had brought them mightily out of Egypt, who had split the Red Sea in two, and who had provided everything they needed. Subsequently, they succumbed to their fears and missed out on God's blessings.

Fear is the biggest reason why someone who isn't apathetic toward the lost and actually *wants* to tell them about Jesus won't. It is the number one thing that keeps us from God's work. It is what paralyzes us from telling the truth about the Lord Jesus Christ.

Fear is the best attack that the devil can launch against you and the primary arrow in his quiver. But the interesting thing is that fear is mostly an illusion. I've heard it described as "(F)alse (E)vidence (A)ppearing (R)eal." It's smoke and mirrors. The devil is a master magician, and fear is his best prop. That's because 90 percent of the things we worry about never happen.

And yet fear stops us from moving forward with so many adventures and countless opportunities that God has set before us. It's the source of the excuses we give for not sharing our faith:

I'm shy.

I'm scared.

I don't know what to say.
It's difficult.
I'm not gifted enough.

So how do we get past our fear of sharing the gospel? How do we disarm that which tries desperately to prevent us from seeing the great blessing of valuable souls won to Christ? Allow me to share seven ways you can fight fear for good:

#1 and #2—Prayer and the Holy Spirit

First, we must know as believers that we cannot accomplish anything worthwhile without prayer and the Holy Spirit—and evangelism is no exception to this rule. I call it "the dynamic duo." The next chapter is dedicated to studying how prayer and the Holy Spirit are essential to sharing your faith. Both are truly your secret weapons in the battle for lost souls.

When you are faithful in prayer, with the Holy Spirit's help, you will find strength and boldness you never imagined. Fear won't have a foothold! As a result, you will see lives transformed for Christ and His glory.

#3—Adopt God's Appraisal

Understanding the value of one soul is a huge motivator in helping us push past our fear—just like my father was able to spring into action that day and rescue my sister from drowning. If we could begin to see every person we come across as an invaluable soul with an eternal destiny, it would change everything. Billy Graham wrote,

> The soul longs for God. Down deep inside every person's heart is a cry for something, but he doesn't quite know what it is. Man is a worshiping creature. He instinctively

knows that there is something out there somewhere, and he longs to know that something or someone. Your soul longs for vital contact with God. Your soul is valuable because it is eternal—it is forever.[2]

The lost are of inestimable worth to God. This becomes astonishingly clear as we read through Luke 15, where Jesus shared the parables of the lost sheep, the lost coin, and the lost son. The Pharisees and the teachers of the law disdained the fact that Jesus welcomed tax collectors and sinners. Knowing this, Jesus told three stories to help them understand God's heart for people whom the Pharisees didn't think were worthy. In each story, Jesus told of the great lengths to which each person went in order to find that which was lost.

Sheep—Surely Jesus's audience could relate to the value of sheep. Domestic sheep were of great importance in biblical times. "Herds of sheep formed the greater part of the wealth of the Patriarchs. The chief animal of sacrifice, and valued for both milk and wool. Sheepskins were made into rough coats. The horns were used as vessels for carrying liquids, particularly oil."[3]

So Jesus asked the Pharisees and teachers of the law to ponder owning a hundred sheep and asked what a shepherd would do if one sheep went missing. "Doesn't he leave the ninety-nine in the open country and go after the lost sheep until he finds it? And when he finds it, he joyfully puts it on his shoulders and goes home. Then he calls his friends and neighbors together and says, 'Rejoice with me; I have found my lost sheep.'"

Coins—Then He asked them to consider a woman who owned ten silver coins and lost one. Jesus probably was referring to silver coins called "drachma." They were worth the equivalent of a denarius, about a day's wages for the common laborer. That was a lot of money back then! Jesus asked, "Doesn't she light a lamp, sweep the house and search carefully until she finds it? And when she finds it, she calls her friends and neighbors together and says, 'Rejoice with me; I have found my lost coin.'"

After these first two parables, Jesus revealed something powerful: "In the same way, I tell you, there is rejoicing in the presence of the angels of God over one sinner who repents." Why would all of heaven be exuberantly happy over a repentant sinner? Because lost souls matter to God!

A Prodigal Son—To drive home this point, Jesus told them a third parable of a prodigal son who asked his father for his inheritance early. You remember the story, right? The young man left home and squandered his wealth on foolish pleasures. Humiliated and starving, he was literally living in a pigsty—and the pigs were eating better than he was! So he came to his senses and decided to return home and beg his father for forgiveness. He intended to ask his father if he could become one of his father's hired servants.

But the Bible says the dad was filled with compassion, ran to his son—which in that time and culture would have been an act of major humility—and hugged and kissed him.

The son said to him, "Father, I have sinned against heaven and against you. I am no longer worthy to be called your son."

But the father said to his servants, "Quick! Bring the best robe and put it on him. Put a ring on his finger and sandals on his feet. Bring the fattened calf and kill it. Let's have a feast and celebrate. For this son of mine was dead and is alive again; he was lost and is found." So they began to celebrate.

Rejoice. Rejoice. Celebrate. Over and over again in these parables we see the great mercy of our God toward sinners—and His unbridled *joy* when they repent. The lost are valuable to Him.

#4—Understand Satan Set His Sights

But the lost are valuable to Satan as well. We learn in 1 Peter 5:8 that "the devil prowls around like a roaring lion looking for someone to devour." I think of a bounty hunter who travels across state lines to hunt down a fugitive because there is a price on that person's head. That fugitive is worth that bounty hunter's time and energy because there is a monetary reward to be gained.

Have you ever been at a pool party and someone pushes you into the pool? When that happens, even though you are caught off guard, what do you do instinctively? You try to grab the person who pushed you and anyone else standing nearby to pull them into the pool with you! The devil is going to hell (Matthew 25:41), and he wants to take everyone with him.

Satan has set his sights on the lost, but we don't have to sit on the sidelines. Knowing that souls are precious helps us get involved in the fight by sharing Jesus with as many people as possible in our lifetime.

#5—He, Not We

In Judges chapter 6, we are introduced to a fearful follower named Gideon. He lived during a very difficult time in Israel's history. Israel had done evil in the sight of the Lord, so God allowed the Midianites to oppress them for seven years. Every time the Israelites would plant crops, the Midianites—who were too numerous to count—would come down and destroy them. The Midianites would destroy Israel's sheep, cattle, and donkeys as well.

One day the angel of the Lord appeared to Gideon and said, "The LORD is with you, mighty warrior." It's interesting that the angel called Gideon this, because it seems that Gideon was far from mighty. We see from the text that he was actually quite afraid, timid, and doubtful. But perhaps the title had less to do with who Gideon was at that moment than who he would later become. More importantly, the angel of the Lord put the emphasis on *God* from the get-go by saying, "The LORD is with you."

Gideon questioned and doubted a little more, and then the Lord said to him, "Go in the strength you have and save Israel out of Midian's hand. Am I not sending you?"

"Pardon me, my lord," Gideon said, "but how can I save Israel? My clan is the weakest in Manasseh, and I am the least in my family." The Lord answered, "I will be with you, and you will strike down all the Midianites, leaving none alive" (vv. 11–16).

Like we often do when confronted with a challenge, Gideon kept thinking about himself—his inabilities, his lack of qualifications, his past, his weaknesses. But each time God rightly turned the focus on Himself—His abilities, His faithfulness, His purpose, and His incomparable strength.

God is also trustworthy (Psalm 28:6–7), and when it comes to sharing our faith, we can trust Him to lead and guide us. We can trust God to send out His Word and that it will not return void (Isaiah 55:11). In the battle for lost souls, may we remember that it's all about "He," not "we."

#6—Redefine Courage

The definition of courage has gotten confused and diluted over the years. Being courageous does not mean taking a popular cultural stance and receiving cheers, accolades, media coverage, or endorsements. We see this often in our world today, but the thing is, having courage rarely comes with reward or applause. It is doing what is right in the face of adversity—with no concern for one's own well-being or the opinions of others.

I also want to dispel the misconception that courage is something you're born with. While it is true that some people seem more outgoing or adventurous by nature, those are personality traits.

Courage, however, is a choice.

It can be developed over time and with the right mind-set. Maya Angelou once said, "One isn't necessarily born with courage, but one is born with potential. Without courage, we cannot practice any other virtue with consistency."[4]

The fact that you have come this far through this book is proof of your potential and desire to tell someone about Jesus. Now you must move from what you know in your mind and heart to action, and that takes courage.

If your heart thumps hard against your rib cage and your palms get sweaty, that's okay! I don't think there's a single skydiver on the planet who doesn't have butterflies in their stomach right before they're about to jump from a plane. But when you are passionate about something, you push past that anxiety because you know it's only temporary—and what you're about to do is far greater than momentary feelings or emotions, or even pain.

In 2 Corinthians 11:24–28, we see that Paul endured extreme suffering for the gospel. His is a compelling example of risk for modern-day Christians:

- Five times he received thirty-nine lashes from the Jews. Three times he was beaten with rods. Once he was pelted with stones. Three times he was shipwrecked. He spent a day and a night in the open sea.
- He was constantly on the move.

- He faced danger from rivers, bandits, fellow Jews, Gentiles, and false believers. He faced danger in the city and in the country.
- He worked hard and often went without sleep.
- He knew hunger and thirst.
- He endured the cold and nakedness.
- He faced the daily pressure of his concern for all the churches.

By faith, Paul had the courage to risk life and limb—literally—in order to deliver the gospel. To save souls. Do we care about the eternal fate of unbelievers as much as he did? American Christians usually only have to worry about possible ridicule or rejection. Perhaps that fear of taking risks is why we are not seeing as many lives changed for Christ as we could be.

Instead, let us become inspired by Paul, who was unconcerned for his own well-being and traveled the world teaching the good news to others who, in turn, taught others. And they, in turn, taught others. Courage is a choice, and it is one reason why the gospel continues to spread even today.

#7—Practice Perfects Your Witnessing Skills

When you choose to share your faith, you will learn and grow from each experience. And you'll get better with practice.

My first ministry after college was in Des Moines, Iowa, where I became good buddies with a guy named Chris. He was also a young pastor. We were both single at the time, and we were always hanging out together.

One day we came up with a dare. Wherever we were, when one of us pointed out a person, the other had to go up and witness to them right then and there. We took turns with this. If it was Chris's turn, he'd point out someone to me, and I'd have to go and introduce myself to the person. Then I'd tell them I was from the local church and talk to them about Jesus and the Bible.

As it often happens with young men, it didn't take long before our little game became a full-fledged competition. We would take turns challenging the other person to share the gospel with a stranger, and each time we would try to find a person who appeared the most difficult to approach.

On one occasion Chris and I drove past a house that we both were convinced was haunted. It was an old house with an unkempt yard filled with every kind of antique you can imagine. During Christmas, the owner of the house would string corn cob Christmas lights on his house. Whatever person lived in the house would certainly be unique. Of this, there was no doubt.

> Let us become inspired by Paul, who was unconcerned for his own well-being and traveled the world teaching the good news to others who, in turn, taught others.

As we were passing by the house, it happened to be my turn to pick. I turned to Chris with a big grin on my face and brought the car to a stop in front of the haunted house.

My friend's shoulders hung low. But he did it. He went up and knocked on the door and spoke with the old man who lived there for a while and then came back to the car. When he got back in, he said, "That was the strangest person I ever met."

Nothing crazy happened, and I'm not sure whether the old man from the spooky house ever accepted Jesus, but what was so important about our evangelism challenges was this: we were learning how to get past that initial fear, jump into an unknown situation, and talk to people about the gospel. By practicing our evangelism, not only were we actively sharing the truth of Jesus

Christ, but we were also getting braver and braver the more we tried. After a while, it wasn't such a big deal.

The first time you attempt to dive into a pool it can be scary! But the more you do it, the better you become. The initial fear of the unknown dissipates because you have invaluable experience under your belt. You might find you actually *enjoy* that activity. It may even become rewarding to you!

Chris and I jumped into the pool of sharing the gospel. Of course we felt pangs of fear at the prospect of being yelled at or mocked for our faith. Of course we worried that we might fail. But we couldn't let that anxiety get in the way of what we were called to do. And the more we spoke with people, the easier it became to get past that fear. This practice affected our ministries for years to come, making us into the bold preachers we are today.

My father was more than courageous that fateful day at the park. He was motivated by immeasurable love and understood how precious my sister's life was. So much so that he dropped his plate and ran and launched into the pond to save her.

Friend, this is exactly how we must feel about the people around us every day. There are precious souls who are lost in this world and without hope for eternity with Jesus Christ. They are drowning. But unlike my sister, Debbie, they might not even know it! It's up to you and it is up to me to extend our arm—with the saving knowledge of the truth—and extract them from that slippery, miry, mossy lake of eternal separation of God.

I ask you, what could be worth more than the value of a soul? What could be more rewarding than seeing a person come to Christ? For such a great reward, should we not risk everything?

Shouldn't we risk our pride, feelings, reputation, and comfort to tell as many people as possible about who He is and how much He loves them?

Each and every person on earth is valuable to God. He risked His one and only Son, Jesus, to save the entire world. It's been said that if you were the only person on earth, Jesus *still* would have undergone His suffering and crucifixion so that you could spend eternity with Him.

When fear creeps up in your mind and tries to prevent you from your sharing your faith with someone, say to yourself, "This person is worth it." Then tell your fear to go take a hike.

Now let's dive into the dynamic duo—prayer and the Holy Spirit—which will further embolden you to step outside of your comfort zone, put courage into practice, and step out in faith.

DISCUSSION QUESTIONS

1. Has there ever been a time when fear prevented you from doing something important? What were you afraid of in that instance?

2. What does 1 Peter 3:14–15 instruct believers to do? How does this passage encourage you during difficult times as a Christian?

3. What do Romans 8:37, 1 Thessalonians 5:5, and 1 Peter 2:9 reveal about how God views you? How do these words help you to overcome your fears?

4. Which of the seven methods of overcoming fear in this chapter do you most connect with? Write out some ways in which that method will help you to share the gospel.

5. Read 1 John 4:18. How can God's perfect love drive out our fear?

6. How does the value of the souls of family members, friends, coworkers, or even strangers you've never met, compel you to move past your fear and share the love of Christ with them?

CHAPTER 6

The Dynamic Duo

"The story of Christian reformation, revival,
and renaissance underscores that the darkest hour
is often just before the dawn, so we should always
be people of hope and prayer, not gloom and defeatism.
God the Holy Spirit can turn the situation
around in five minutes."

OS GUINNESS

The only memory I have of my paternal grandfather was when my father took me to the hospital one snowy night to visit him before he died. I was four years old. I didn't get the chance to know my grandfather, but I got to know my grandmother very well. She used to tell me all kinds of stories about my grandfather. I could sit and listen to her stories for hours. But one story was my favorite, and she could never tell it to me enough times.

When my grandmother met my grandfather, he was a lawyer for the United States government, working in Tulsa, Oklahoma. When they met and fell in love, he did what every respectable young man in that day would do: he took her home to meet his mother. But my grandfather had to warn my grandmother about something.

"Millie, I'm taking you home to introduce you to my mom," he said. "As soon as you walk in the door, she's gonna tell you, 'My son Jimmy is gonna be a preacher one day.'"

After my grandmother recovered from the initial shock—after all, lawyers are not often compelled to become preachers—my grandfather began to explain how, as a little boy, he became deathly ill. This was back before the days of modern medicine, so when a child got sick it could be a very hopeless situation. His mother prayed, "God, if You take my little boy, I will understand. But if You would somehow heal little Jimmy, he will grow up and be a great preacher and a great man of God one day."

And God answered her prayers.

My grandfather began to get better instantly and within a few days was completely healed. Staying true to her promise, his mother soon began to introduce her boy by saying, "This is my son Jimmy. He's gonna be a preacher one day."

It didn't make any difference whom he was being introduced to; my grandfather's mother would always say the same thing over, and over, and over again. During his elementary and junior high years, my grandfather was afraid to bring anyone home from school because he knew what his mom would announce right as his guest walked in the door.

Now in his thirties and bringing home his wife-to-be, it would be no different. The same scenario. Nothing had changed. The greeting was going to be what it had been for the last twenty-five years. My grandmother told me that when they walked through that door, just like clockwork, the first words she heard were:

"Hi, Millie. Nice to meet you. Did you know that Jimmy's gonna be a preacher one day?"

After they were married, my grandfather and grandmother attended a very small church that probably had no more than thirty people on their best Sunday. The pastor left suddenly, and they were without a preacher. The elders approached my grandfather and asked him if he would be interested in doing some of the preaching. Of course his response was, "I'm in the law business, and I know nothing, absolutely nothing, about preaching."

But my grandmother had another reaction. She said, "James, let's pray about this," and then told the elders, "Give us two weeks to pray, and then we will let you know."

I can only imagine the reaction of my grandfather at that moment!

After what I'm sure seemed like the longest two weeks in his life, my grandfather went to the elders and committed to preach for two weeks. My grandmother said his exact words were: "Two weeks. I will preach two weeks only. That will be it, and don't ever ask me again."

He did, in fact, preach those two weeks . . . and the next week . . . and the next week . . . and the next week. By the time it was all said and done, my grandfather was the pastor of that church for almost thirty years! He built the largest Christian church in Oklahoma at that time. Even though he became a great soul winner for his generation, his greatest legacy is found in his three children who became preachers, including my father, who preached for close to seventy years. And here I am, a grandson, a third-generation preacher whose three children are also serving the Lord. All because of the faithful prayers of one woman—a great-grandmother I never met, but whose prayers changed four generations!

Prayer Is the Key

The beautiful thing about prayer is that it can break down any obstacle, open any door, and change any circumstance. When you are compelled to tell others about Jesus, prayer is the key God has given you to unlock the doors of opportunity and to allow you to walk right into your divine appointment.

This truth is exemplified in the life of John Hyde, the son of a Presbyterian minister, who moved to India in 1892. At that time he was one of only five known Christian missionaries in a region consisting of nearly one million non-Christians. Physically challenged through partial deafness, John Hyde soon realized something that was stronger than his weakness:

The power of prayer.

After many years of very little success and very few conversions to Christ, John Hyde began to pray what many thought to be an impossible request: "God, give me one soul today." Because of his dismal beginnings as a missionary, this prayer seemed to be asking for the entire world. But he just wanted to lead one soul to Jesus Christ every day. All throughout the year, he kept track, and at the end of the 1908, he had in fact led over four hundred people to Jesus Christ.

That was just the beginning for John Hyde.

In 1909, he prayed that God would give him *two* souls every single day. Not only did he ask God to double his efforts, but John Hyde also doubled his prayer time. Again, at the end of that year, his figures showed some eight hundred people who had accepted Jesus as their Savior. By 1910, John Hyde's commitment

> When you are compelled to tell others about Jesus, prayer is the key God has given you to unlock the doors of opportunity and to allow you to walk right into your divine appointment.

to prayer and his reputation earned him the nickname "Praying John Hyde." His fervent prayer became known throughout the Christian community worldwide:

Give me souls, O God, or I die! God, give me souls!

In 1910, he once again asked God for double: *four* souls a day. Nothing less. God was once again faithful to answer his prayer, and over 1,600 people came to salvation during that year!

A few years later, John Hyde died. The medical examiner discovered something truly amazing. His heart had literally shifted in his chest cavity, moving from the left side of his body to the right. There was no logical medical explanation for this phenomenon.[1] However, many believed this was partially due to the intense burden of prayer that was laid upon his heart.

The life of "Praying John Hyde" is more than just a good story; it is a true-life example of the spiritual effectiveness that is released when prayer is combined with the leading of the Holy Spirit. John Hyde translated his burden for the lost into commitment, time, prayer, and a daily reliance on God's faithfulness. Each and every morning you and I can adopt his same passionate plea, "God, give me souls!" and watch and see what God will do.

Who's on Your List?

When I was in college, there was a professor who told us he had prayed for his mother to be saved every day . . . for fifty years! One day the professor walked into our class and said that over the weekend, his mom had accepted Jesus as her Savior and was baptized. She was ninety-six years old! I will never forget the expression of joy on his face. All of the days, hours, months, and years of prayer suddenly all came to fruition.

That motivated me to action. From that time on, I started a list of names of people I pray will be saved, and I have encouraged many others to do the same.

During a lunch meeting with all of our pastors one day, I asked them to think of someone they could never imagine getting saved. I wanted them to think big. Relatives who seem adamantly against Christianity. Friends who have rejected every invitation to church. International icons—superstars, athletes, and political figures—who don't know the Lord. Once the guys were finished brainstorming, we went around and shared a few of the names each person had written on their list.

Then I encouraged the men by saying, "Now pray for that list every day."

It was a great reminder, even for us pastors, that prayer can make an eternal difference in someone's life. Some of us are still praying for the people on our lists all these years later. Sean's grandfather. Jeremy's college roommate and longtime friend. Salvation is possible for every single person—no matter how impossible it may seem.

Maybe at some point in your life *you* were that impossible person. But aren't you glad that someone put you on their list one day? It could have been a family member, a Sunday school teacher, a friend, a neighbor, or someone you don't even know. Most likely someone was praying for your salvation.

Can you imagine how the world would be transformed if only Christians would get on their knees every morning and zealously pray for every person in their life to be saved? I believe the best way to begin this prayer movement is to reflect back on the names you wrote down in chapter 1 and carve out some time each day to pray for these five people. Start today. Pray that God would prepare their hearts, that He would open their eyes to the truth, and that He would provide an opportunity for you to share the gospel with them.

You might even tell the person months from now, "Hey, I just want you to know that I've been praying for you every day." You'd be amazed how surprising that may be to some people, and how touched they may be to know that you care.

What Happens When You Pray?

God hears your prayers. Pray boldly. Pray consistently. It could make an eternal difference in a person's life—even if it takes fifty years, as in the case of my college professor's mother.

Let's take a look at four spectacular things that happen when the component of prayer begins to be activated in your life:

1. Prayer Will Shift Your Heart

Complacency and apathy have no place in the hearts of those whose lives have been radically transformed by Jesus. We must carry a deep concern for those who are lost and spend time in prayer for them. When you pray earnestly for people who need salvation, something begins to shift inside your heart—just as it did, literally, for dear John Hyde.

Paul was also very passionate about prayer. In Romans 10:1, he wrote, "Brothers and sisters, my heart's desire and prayer to God for the Israelites is that they may be saved." In Romans 9:3–4, he made a stunning statement that he was willing to be cursed and go to hell forever if through that one decision, his entire brethren would come to know Jesus Christ. Later, we learn in Ephesians 3:8–9 and Galatians 2:9 that God appointed Paul to bring the gospel to the Gentiles (everyone who is not Jewish by birth). And in 1 Timothy 2:1–4, Paul urged believers to pray to God on behalf of *all* people—whether they are in high positions or low.

John Hyde and the apostle Paul teach us that prayer nurtures, develops, and increases the burden in our heart for lost people. Today, would you say this prayer? "God, please forgive me because I have been indifferent to the lost people around me. Please shift my heart to be like Yours, deeply concerned for those who need salvation. In Jesus's name, I pray. Amen."

2. Prayer Opens the Doors of Opportunity

Have you ever wanted to share your faith with someone but you felt as though there was a wall standing between you and that person? Or perhaps you've tried, and you end up feeling as though a door was slammed in your face. (Or maybe a door was literally slammed in your face!) I'm sure many Christians have experienced this, and it's easy to become discouraged or lose hope that you can make a difference. But let's examine for a moment a key in Colossians 4:3. Toward the end of his letter to the believers living in Colossae, Paul wrote, "And pray for us, too, that God may open a door for our message, so that we may proclaim the mystery of Christ . . ."

Prayer is the key to opening new doors of opportunity to share the gospel. We know that God opened the door for Paul to share the good news with both Jews and Gentiles, women, men, prison guards, and kings. I believe that it pleases the Lord when we pray and ask Him to open the door for His message of truth. We demonstrate our willingness to be used as His vessels. I also believe God will respond in a powerful way by opening doors, moving things around behind the scenes, and providing a way where no way seemed possible before.

3. Prayer Gives You Boldness

When doors of opportunity open, not everyone is ready to charge through them. Some people wouldn't hesitate to move forward at the sight of a divine appointment unfolding before their eyes. But others could find themselves in a Jonah type of response—hightailing it in the opposite direction! We discussed in the last chapter that the number one thing that keeps people from sharing their faith is fear. But the good news is, not only does a life of prayer open doors, but it also gives you a supernatural dose of boldness to *carpe diem*—seize the day!

This is exactly what happened to the disciples right after Jesus was taken up to heaven. The Bible says in Acts 4:31, "After they prayed, the place where they were meeting was shaken. And they were all filled with the Holy Spirit and spoke the word of God boldly."

In Ephesians 6:19, Paul urged the church at Ephesus to pray for him that he would boldly fearlessly preach the gospel. Like a fresh, bubbling spring of water, boldness to speak God's Word will flow from the inside of you when you pray. Then those divine intersections become a lot less scary and much more inviting!

4. Prayer Will Give You the Words to Say

Okay, so now you've got a heart that's burdened for the lost. God has opened the door of opportunity to share His message, and He's given you boldness through prayer. What are you going to say to someone who needs Christ? We find one of the greatest encouragements with regard to this question in Isaiah 50:4:

> The Sovereign Lord has given me a well-instructed tongue,
> to know the word that sustains the weary.

He wakens me morning by morning,
>   wakens my ear to listen like one being instructed.

God will instruct your tongue to speak exactly the right words to those who are weary and weak in spirit! What an incredible promise! This type of divine instruction comes by two actions. First, by spending time in God's Word. Second, by praying and asking God to give you the right words to say. Like Isaiah, morning by morning may you wake up with the desire to hear from the Lord as He instructs your tongue what to say.

--- - — ———— — - --

I hope this section has inspired you to activate your prayer life when it comes to evangelism. Because I've witnessed the power of prayer firsthand, I'm so excited about what God is going to do in you, and in others through you, when you begin to pray for the lost! But prayer is only half of the dynamic duo. The counterpart to prayer is the work of the Holy Spirit, which will not only embolden you to share your faith, but also provide a constant comfort and companion.

The Holy Spirit: Our Forgotten Friend?

Imagine you are driving home one night and you run out of gas. To make matters worse, your cell phone is dead so you can't call a friend or AAA to help. You realize your only choice is to walk a few blocks to the nearest gas station. With a deep sigh, you get out of your car and begin the trek. You can see the lights ahead for the gas station, but you have to walk through a dark alley in order to get there.

It looks scary. You don't know who or what may be lurking, and you begin to worry, *What if I get robbed or attacked?* You stop for a moment to consider your choices: you can either walk through the alley and hope for the best, or you can go back to your vehicle and sit there until daylight.

Now, what if I told you that you had a companion there with you who happened to be a Mixed Martial Arts (MMA) champion . . . or a Navy SEAL . . . or Chuck Norris? How does this change the scene in your mind? I would bet you wouldn't be afraid to walk down that dark alley. My guess is you would have all the confidence in the world.

When it comes to sharing the gospel, we wrestle with intimidation, insecurity, and outright fear. But the truth is, you're not alone! The Holy Spirit is with you at all times, to fill you with courage and give you the words to say.

> The work of delivering the gospel is not mine alone. It is shared by the Spirit of the Living God who will empower, encourage, and enable me to deliver His message.

Jesus told His disciples in Luke 12:11–12, "When you are brought before synagogues, rulers and authorities, do not worry about how you will defend yourselves or what you will say, for the Holy Spirit will teach you at that time what you should say."

This verse lifts a massive burden from my shoulders. The work of delivering the gospel is not mine alone. It is shared by the Spirit of the Living God who will empower, encourage, and enable me to deliver His message.

What Does the Holy Spirit Do?

When my children were little, I used to take them fishing at a lake just outside of town. Once we got there, I would do all the work. I would bait the hook for them, cast it out into the water for them, and then we would wait until a fish took a bite.

All they had to do was hold the pole. It was their only job. They didn't have to fiddle with the lure or put a slimy worm on the hook. They didn't have to cast the line into the lake. They just had to hold the pole. Once they got a bite, I would even help them reel in their catch.

Isn't that similar to what God does for us when it comes to soul winning? We often make evangelism much harder than it needs to be, inviting unnecessary fear into our souls. But in reality, God does most of the work for us; He's just asking us to participate with Him in the process. As Jesus said in John 15:5, "I am the vine; you are the branches. If you remain in me and I in you, you will bear much fruit; apart from me you can do nothing."

That doesn't mean God will do *everything* for you. On the contrary, God pulls us into the process and works through us in order to spread His message. And He does all of this by His Spirit, who dwells within us.

In those moments when I am not sure what to say, the Spirit comes alongside me and enables me to speak. He works in me while I'm sharing the message, and—at the exact same time—He works in those who are listening. He is the grand conductor, orchestrating a plan that leads us all to salvation.

Here are four important ways the Holy Spirit works and give us courage to face our fears:

1. He Prepares

Do you realize that, right now, the Holy Spirit is at work? Right where you are, God is stirring the hearts of those who are looking for answers and searching for hope. The Holy Spirit is preparing them for the truth of God's Word.

The question is, are you letting the Spirit prepare you as well? Are you seeking the Spirit in prayer? Are you diving into God's

Word to see how you can grow? Are you allowing the Spirit to work as a refining fire within you?

If you allow Him, the Spirit will mold you and form you in order to bear His message without fear. Ephesians 2:10 declares, "For we are God's handiwork, created in Christ Jesus to do good works, which God prepared in advance for us to do." God has not only prepared works in advance for us to do, but He also prepares *us* for that good work.

This is wonderful news—and there's more!

When admonishing Christians to put on the full armor of God, the King James Version of the Bible says the feet of Christians are to be "shod with the preparation of the gospel of peace" (Ephesians 6:15). You see, the gospel has already been prepared! This part of the armor covers our feet because we are supposed to go, to walk, to move, to travel with the good news, taking it to others who need it. It's ready for the sharing, and the Holy Spirit is readying you!

2. He Positions

Has a friend ever called you out of the blue and encouraged you when you really needed it? Has a stranger ever shown you kindness or given you much-needed advice? Maybe you received something you needed but hadn't asked for?

The world thinks these types of things happen on accident or by coincidence, but I believe that when a specific incident has spiritual and/or eternal implications, it's a divine appointment. It's the coming together of the right people, at the right time, in the right place, for the right reason. We gain greater insight into this topic from Acts 17:26–27. In an impassioned speech to the people of Athens who had been following after false gods, Paul said this:

From one man [God] made all the nations, that they should

inhabit the whole earth; and he marked out their appointed times in history and the boundaries of their lands. God did this so that they would seek him and perhaps reach out for him and find him, though he is not far from any one of us.

Throughout history, God has appointed our "when" and positioned our "where." We can find biblical examples of when the Lord did this in more specific ways: David, as the chosen king of Israel; Esther saving her people; Jonah's mission to Nineveh; the prophets of the Old Testament; Ananias healing Saul and proclaiming Jesus as Lord; Paul and the Philippian jailer; Philip and the Ethiopian eunuch—the list goes on and on.

So we see that the Holy Spirit not only prepares us to be used by God and to share His message, but also places us in a position to do just that!

3. He Empowers

What do you think of when you hear the word *dynamite*? Perhaps a bundle of red sticks and a ticking clock, like in the old cartoons? The word usually carries with it images of explosion, force, and strength. Everything about dynamite is connected to power.

In the book of Acts, Jesus made an incredible promise right before He was taken up into heaven. He said, "But you will receive power when the Holy Spirit comes on you; and you will be my witnesses in Jerusalem, and in all Judea and Samaria, and to the ends of the earth" (1:8).

The word *power* in this verse comes from the Greek word *dunamis*.[2] You've probably guessed by now that *dunamis* is translated into "dynamite" in English. The very last thing Jesus said on earth was that the Holy Spirit was going to infuse believers with "dynamic power." In other words, we have dynamite in us! That dynamite is just waiting to be released—resulting in you telling someone about Jesus. When you accepted Jesus as your Savior, you were filled with the Holy Spirit. And at that very moment, you were filled with spiritual power. You became walking dynamite!

The Holy Spirit is preparing, positioning, and empowering you for a specific purpose: to be a witness for Christ in the world! He is the dynamic spiritual force that enables you to push past your fear and share your faith—even when you feel you can't. Every believer, not just pastors, has the responsibility to unleash this power from God!

4. He Comforts

The last thing I want to share with you about the Holy Spirit has to do with *who* the Holy Spirit is. I understand that even among Christians there's a lot of mystery concerning the Holy Spirit, but Jesus didn't leave us wondering. He explained very clearly the identity of the Holy Spirit in John 14:26. I like the way it's stated in this Bible version:

> But the Helper (Comforter, Advocate, Intercessor—Counselor, Strengthener, Standby), the Holy Spirit, whom the Father will send in My name [in My place, to represent Me and act on My behalf], He will teach you all things. And He will help you remember everything that I have told you. (AMP)

As a believer in Christ, as you witness to others and in everything you do, you have a highly capable and qualified helper with you at all times. Whether someone rejects or disappoints you, and whether you encounter sorrows or hardships, the Holy Spirit will comfort you. He is also your advocate and intercessor, which means He defends you and speaks on your behalf. He is your strengthener and your standby, which means He is a reliable support always. How many times have you been able to recall a Bible verse at just the right time? That's the Holy Spirit too. Jesus said He would help us remember everything He told His followers. What a wonderful friend we have in Him.

Prayer and the Holy Spirit are two very powerful forces. When we put them together in our walk with Christ and in our desire to witness to others, it's a game changer. I hope you will always remember that God has given you this dynamic duo to be cherished and utilized each and every day.

Are you feeling pumped? Do you feel like you're ready to take on the world with these two awesome gifts and everything we've learned so far? Great! Let's now move from the "why" of evangelism to the "how" in the next chapter.

DISCUSSION QUESTIONS

1. How was your trust and faith built up in God through the answering of prayer?

2. How do you think the Holy Spirit changes our hearts and minds as we pray for others rather than for ourselves?

3. Read John 14:26. According to this verse, what are some of the duties of the Holy Spirit in our lives? How have you seen or experienced the Holy Spirit prepare, position, empower, and comfort you during your journey with God?

4. Read Acts 2:1–4; 4:1–13; 8:26–40; and 16:16–34. How do we see the Holy Spirit take over the lives of the disciples throughout these verses and, really, the entire book of Acts?

5. All of us are uniquely created and designed by God to serve in His kingdom. In what ways does the Holy Spirit compel you to share the gospel of Jesus in the unique manner that God has created you?

CHAPTER 7

Mouth-to-Ear Resuscitation

"There is no greater honor than to be the instrument
in God's hands of leading one person
out of the kingdom of Satan
into the glorious light of Heaven."

DWIGHT L. MOODY

Several summers ago I spent a week by myself at a friend's time-share in Hawaii and planned the preaching schedule for the following year at our church. Every morning I walked down to the beach from the condo. I'd take my briefcase and my study notes and sit on a chair in the sand. The entire week I was there I would occasionally look up from my work and watch the surfers in the ocean.

I had never been surfing before. I kept looking at the people paddling out and catching waves, and I felt like it was something I could do. I'd watch for a little while, but then I'd go back to my studies.

On Wednesday of that week, I was walking down the main street of Waikiki in super-casual vacation mode. I hate to tell you this, but I'm not sure I even had a shirt on. I didn't think I would run into anyone who knew me. Suddenly a car pulled over and I heard, "Pastor Dudley! Pastor Dudley!"

I peered inside the car and sitting inside was a married couple from Shepherd Church, along with their two children in the backseat. They were smiling and waving at me.

I said, "Hi! How are ya?"

They slowed down, and it seemed like they were going to talk to me, but the drivers in the cars behind them started to honk their horns. The family drove off, and for the rest of the week I kept looking for them but couldn't find them.

Back at my portable workstation on the beach, I'd glance up at the surfers and think, *This is the day I'm gonna surf.* But I'd sit down on that chair with my Bible and my papers and quickly my entire day would fill up with work.

Finally it was Friday. The last day of my trip. I decided I was going to go surfing. At least I was going to try. As I walked down to the little bungalow where you could rent surfboards, I noticed a big sign that read, "DO NOT ENTER THE OCEAN—JELLYFISH WARNING."

I just looked at the sign and prayed, "Lord, is this You telling me I'm not supposed to go surfing by myself?"

There was a police officer standing there, so I said to him, "Are there really jellyfish out there?"

He replied, "Oh yeah. We've treated about forty-five people this morning already. You don't wanna go out in the ocean."

I said, "You mean you would advise me not to go?"

And he said, "If I were you, I wouldn't go. I'd pick another day."

So I went back to my chair and sat down. But out in the ocean there were still a few people surfing despite the jellyfish warning. Afternoon rolled around and I thought, *You know what? I can do this. I don't care if there are jellyfish in the ocean; I'm going surfing.*

I rented a surfboard that was about ten feet long, and smack-dab in the middle of the board was a big Star of David. Of all the boards the rental guy could have given me, that was the one he picked. So I took it as a sign from the Lord, telling me I was supposed to go out there and surf that day.

The guy gave me a short lesson. I laid my giant surfboard on the sand, and he instructed me to kneel down on the board. He said, "When you get out there, you've gotta paddle real hard with both hands. Then you gotta jump up. I'm gonna say, 'Go.' See if you can jump up and land on the board."

He said, "Go!" And I jumped up and stood on the board.

So the instructor said, "Hey, you're ready to go! Just do that out there, and you'll be fine."

I awkwardly carried my board out to the shore and thought, *Lord, am I supposed to be doing this?* As soon as I took a step into the water, a big wave came up and knocked down a lady who was carrying her surfboard. When she fell, her surfboard swung around and hit me in my shin.

Now I was *limping* into the ocean, thinking, *Lord, is this a sign that I'm not supposed to go out there?*

I gave myself another pep talk and headed out into the ocean once again. Because of the jellyfish, I had to lie flat on the surfboard while trying to look up the entire time instead of the more comfortable position of sitting up on the board with my legs in the ocean. I spent an hour trying to catch a wave. It was hotter than blazes. I would see a wave coming, and even though I tried to stand up on the surfboard again and again, I kept falling into the water. Or I would try to catch a wave but it would go right by me.

It was very discouraging. I got tired. I was getting dehydrated out there in that salt water, and at one point I thought I was going to faint. So I decided to call it a day. I let a wave carry me to the shore, and as I was getting out of the water, I looked over and the guy who was driving the car I saw a couple of days earlier came walking up to me.

I said, "Hey, I've been looking for you guys all week!"

"Oh," he said. "We've been here."

I invited him and his family out to dinner that night. We met up at a Mexican restaurant, and halfway through our conversation, the man said, "You know, we were watching you the entire time you were trying to surf."

"You were?" I exclaimed.

He said, "Yeah, we watched the whole thing. We kept wishing we had a video camera with us."

"Wait a minute," I interjected. "You mean to tell me that you sat on the beach and just watched me for an hour?"

He replied, "Yeah, it was pretty funny."

I said, "Ugh, I can't believe it! All I needed was one guy to come out and give me a little push toward the shore when the wave came. If that had happened, I know I would've got up on that surfboard."

"Well, we thought you didn't wanna be bothered," my new friend explained. "You know, you're on vacation and everything. But it was fun watching ya!"

Then their youngest son, who was about nine or ten years old, chimed in, "Hotel room in Hawaii, $200. Airline ticket to Hawaii, $400. Watching your pastor for an hour trying to surf, priceless!"

"Are you gonna tell this story in church?" the dad asked.

I said, "Yes, I am. I'm going to tell the story about how the pastor was out, struggling for an hour, and all he needed was one guy to push him. And you sat on the beach the entire hour and did not lift a finger to help me. I'm going to tell that story to the church."

And I did a few weeks later!

What Is Evangelism?

When it comes to telling others about Jesus, perhaps you're feeling the way I felt as I contemplated whether or not to try surfing. You look out into the world and see other people sharing their faith—and people getting saved as a result—so you know it's possible. But it's sort of like standing on the shoreline of a great surf break, looking for a sign from God as to whether or not you should actually get in the ocean!

So maybe you try it. And struggle. Or get knocked down. Or feel that you have failed and call it a day.

But sometimes it just takes someone giving you a little push or showing you the mechanics of how it's done so you can be successful. That's what I want to begin to do in this chapter and in subsequent chapters. I want to encourage you and show you the simple mechanics of sharing the gospel.

Let's begin by defining a basic term that most Christians have heard but may have a difficult time understanding its meaning and application. It's the word *evangelism*. This word can conjure up a variety of images and thoughts ranging from world missions to flashy televangelists. Many faithful church members would answer, "Evangelism? Oh, that's something our preacher does on Sunday morning."

Well, yes . . . and no.

Many years ago I heard one of the greatest definitions of evangelism, and to this day it has stuck with me: evangelism is nothing more than mouth-to-ear resuscitation!

What a great yet simple description. The gospel of Jesus comes from your mouth to someone else's ear—and brings life to a spirit who, without Christ, is dead in sin (Ephesians 2:1).

With typical mouth-to-mouth resuscitation or CPR, you don't have to be a doctor or medical expert to administer it. Anyone can do it with the proper training. It's the same thing with sharing the gospel! You don't have to be a preacher or possess a master's degree from a Bible college. Any believer can share the good news—effectively—with the proper training.

I hope you will find in the coming chapters that evangelism is not complex. It doesn't have to be complicated or intimidating. And you can participate in it every single day of your life once you have the right tools. Once you do, you will be able to win souls for the kingdom of God.

What do I mean by that? Well, let's dive into what the Bible says about winning souls and the steps to becoming a soul winner.

Soul Winning Made Simple

You've probably heard the term *soul winner* before, and although we don't see this exact term in the Bible, it most likely comes from two different scriptures. The first is Proverbs 11:30, which says, "The fruit of the righteous is a tree of life, and he who is wise wins souls" (NASB). The second comes from 1 Corinthians 9:19–23, where Paul wrote about humbling himself toward everyone so that he could "win as many as possible." He wrote,

> To the Jews I became like a Jew, to *win* the Jews. To those under the law I became like one under the law (though I myself am not under the law), so as to *win* those under the law. To those not having the law I became like one not having the law (though I am not free from God's law but am under Christ's law), so as to *win* those not having the law.

To the weak I became weak, to *win* the weak. I have become all things to all people so that by all possible means I might *save* some. I do all this for the sake of the gospel, that I may share in its blessings.

Four times in this passage Paul used the word *win*. He was using his influence and background to persuade and convince those around him to accept Jesus Christ as their Lord. He was competing for their souls. Do you think this came easily and without a fight, resistance, or conflict? I don't think so. While recapping his life, one of Paul's last words was that he had "fought the good fight."[1]

Winning souls basically means to lead people to a saving knowledge of the truth. Think of the expression "winning someone over." In that sense, you are convincing someone of something or gaining his or her support. Or consider the saying "winning someone's heart." This has a more intimate meaning of gaining a person's affection or causing them to love you exclusively.

Christian fellowship and community are absolutely important. But what's more important is the church's role to equip its members with the knowledge of the Word of God so that we will boldly engage in the war that is taking place over the souls of mankind.

If you are winning souls, then you are a soul winner. I've often wondered why so many people back away from this term. Maybe it's because the word *winning* constitutes a battle or conflict. I realize our society has fallen into a "can't we all just get along" mentality, but the Bible says that there's a war going on. Not a war against people, but against the dark forces in the spiritual realm (Ephesians 6:12). And these powers are doing everything possible to win this war. That same passage of Scripture, Ephesians 6:10–17, also says that we must put on the full armor of God. We wouldn't need to wear armor if a battle wasn't going on, right?

Here's the thing: the church is not a "bless me" club meant to provide comfortable seats and feel-good messages for its members. Christian fellowship and community are absolutely important. But what's *more* important is the church's role to equip its members with the knowledge of the Word of God so that we will boldly engage in the war that is taking place over the souls of mankind.

Paul was actively engaged in this battle. He was willing to go wherever the Spirit led and was excellent at winning people over for the gospel. Isaiah is another great example. We can also learn a lot from Philip the evangelist in the story of the Ethiopian eunuch in Acts 8. In looking at these great evangelists in the Bible, I've noticed seven distinct traits in those who are compelled to tell others about Christ. Let these begin to shape you into the soul winner God has designed you to be:

1. Surrender Your Heart

When the prophet Isaiah stood trembling in the smoke-filled throne room of God he, "heard the voice of the Lord, saying, 'Whom shall I send? And who will go for us?'" There was zero hesitation as Isaiah quickly responded, "Here am I. Send me!" (Isaiah 6:8).

If you were to ask a child if he or she wanted to go to Disneyland, that child's hand would shoot up into the air faster than you could say, "Mickey Mouse"! And that's exactly what happened with Isaiah. Moments earlier he had seen the majesty of the living God. How could he not eagerly volunteer for whatever mission the Lord had in mind? So God told Isaiah to "Go," and speak on His behalf to the people (vv. 9–10).

Many people today lift their hands in church as an expression of worship to the Lord. It's the universal sign of surrender. But the person who is surrendered to God should be lifting their hands not just in church but wherever they go! There should be something in their heart that says, "Lord, I'm completely Yours. Lead me where You want me to go. Send me to the person You want me to talk to." This is a picture of a surrendered heart.

2. Be Available

Back in Acts 8:26–27, Philip's surrendered heart enabled him to be ready and available when God clearly spoke to him: "'Go south to the road—the desert road—that goes down from Jerusalem to Gaza.' So he started out, and on his way he met an Ethiopian eunuch . . ." A few verses later, the Spirit of the Lord once again told him, "Go to that chariot . . ." (v. 29).

Philip made himself available and obeyed God's direction. Did you know that God is more interested in your availability than your ability? Yes, He can use your talents and education for His kingdom—but first and foremost is your availability.

God sent Philip on a soul-winning journey, and Philip did not have a Bible college or seminary degree! When God said, "Go," it wasn't laden with prerequisites and qualifications. "Go" meant . . . go! He wanted to use Philip just as he was.

I'll be the first to highly recommend biblical education to any believer, but if you feel unqualified to share your faith because of a lack of Bible training—don't worry! Even if you don't know much about the Bible, one thing you *do* know is what God has done for you! When you become available for God to use, you are well on your way to becoming a soul winner.

3. Run, Don't Walk

Whenever I coach youth sports, one of the first things I teach the kids is to run to me as fast as they can—as soon as I call them or make certain hand motions—without any hesitation or distraction (and if you have ever coached little league baseball, you *know* how many distractions there can be!). I tell the children from the first practice to run and not walk. This immediately builds a sense of urgency within our team.

Philip was the same way. As soon as God told him to go to that chariot, the Bible says he ran. He didn't give it some thought, check his calendar, or weigh his options. No, Philip moved as fast as he could to do what God had told him to do. There was a sense of urgency.

Soul winners respond the same way today. When the Holy Spirit says, "Go talk to that person over there about Me," they move, and they move quickly. No hesitation. No distractions. During your meal at your favorite restaurant, God might speak to you about witnessing to your server. Or on your way home at the gas station, you might be prompted to share Christ with the person who is on the other side of the gas pump. Whatever the case may be, be ready and respond promptly. The window of opportunity may be but a brief moment. You never know when it will present itself again.

4. Be Sensitive

The first thing Philip did when he arrived at the place God was leading him to was quite impressive. He listened. The Bible says he "heard the man reading" (Acts 8:30). Before he began sharing anything about Jesus to the Ethiopian, he took the time to listen and hear what his need was.

This type of sensitivity is often lacking within the body of Christ today. Marriages are crying for help, but no one is listening. People are hurting and lonely, but no one hears their cries. Being an effective soul winner means not only listening to those around you but also hearing what is sometimes *not* spoken. This becomes very difficult to do when you are the one doing all the talking! It reminds me of an old children's rhyme that says, "A wise old owl sat on an oak; the more he saw the less he spoke; the less he spoke the more he heard; why aren't we like that wise old bird?"

Be sensitive to those around you. Listen to what their needs really are and be ready to share the answer. That answer, Jesus, is alive inside of you!

5. Be Helpful

Here's a little tip: If you are mean to someone, you are decreasing your effectiveness to share the gospel with that person. On the other hand, helpfulness and kindness can go a long way.

When Philip heard the Ethiopian eunuch reading the Old Testament, the first thing he did was offer his assistance. He asked him, "Do you understand what you are reading?"[2] He didn't get in the man's face and say, "Are you saved? If you were run over by an eighteen-wheel chariot today, would you go straight to hell?" There is a difference between being helpful and obnoxious!

When you genuinely have a heart to help someone, it speaks volumes. It can be as simple as taking dinner to a single mother because she works long hours. Or mowing your elderly neighbor's lawn. Or tutoring a student. These helpful acts are very much part of the soul-winning process because kindness has an interesting way of opening doors and softening hearts.

6. Build Rapport

Building a spiritual relationship with someone doesn't always begin with something spiritual. Some type of bond, trust, or friendship is usually formed before a spiritual connection is made. Obviously there was something in Philip that the Ethiopian man trusted. Think about it. There he was, sitting on his chariot, reading something that was completely foreign to him, when Philip dropped in and offered his assistance. Without even knowing him, this man invited Philip to come and sit on his chariot. It was almost as if Philip's reputation went before him.

What is it about you that people trust? Do your noble reputation and character go before you? Are you building rapport with others through the activities in which you are involved and your areas of expertise? If so, you can make a connection with others and be a living example of the difference Jesus can make in a person's life.

7. Preach Jesus

Eventually there comes a time in the soul-winning process when you're going to have to open your mouth and talk about Jesus. When Philip had finished explaining the Scriptures, the eunuch asked him to explain what he had just finished reading.[3] "Then Philip began with that very passage of Scripture and told him the good news about Jesus" (Acts 8:35).

The groundwork had been laid. Everything had been orchestrated by the Holy Spirit for this one, pivotal moment. Philip recognized his opportunity and was ready to complete his mission. So he shared the gospel with his new friend. He didn't give his own opinions or relay what he had heard someone else say; instead, Philip simply preached Jesus.

And look at the miraculous result: the eunuch believed and at once sought the nearest pool of water for his baptism. Afterward, the Bible says that the Holy Spirit took Philip away from there (the original "Beam me up, Scotty!"), and the Ethiopian eunuch left rejoicing. Why was the eunuch so joyful? Because he was a sinner who had welcomed the message of salvation and was now forgiven and born again.

Today there are people just like the Ethiopian eunuch who are waiting for the same good news. How do you find them? Well, you start with a surrendered, available heart that simply desires to go wherever God is calling. Once God prompts you, it's important that you run where He is sending you, just as Philip did.

Be sensitive to the needs of others and build rapport with them.

And finally, preach Jesus. You can literally open up your Bible and show someone the clear imprint of Jesus Christ as Lord and Savior, prophesied throughout the Old Testament and fulfilled in the New Testament.

"Wait!" you say. "But I don't know how to do that last part!"

If you still feel unequipped to surf and are tempted to run back to the shore—don't worry. Throughout the next few chapters, I am going to show you how to present the gospel to others in a simple and understandable way that will take all the stress and mystery out of this seemingly daunting task. First things first: when you first open your mouth, your tone and attitude can determine how well your message will be received. So let's cover this important topic now.

DISCUSSION QUESTIONS

1. How can building rapport with people help you to better share your story and truth with them? Why does God want us to be in relationship with people? What do relationships do to strengthen God's kingdom and His church?

2. What relationships do you already have that need to be built up so that you may be in a position of love and trust to share the gospel?

3. How does this chapter serve as an aid to what you already knew about evangelism? What is something new that you learned from reading this chapter?

4. In this chapter, beginning on page 113, I mentioned seven traits of evangelism in the Bible. How do these traits serve as reminders and/or instructions for telling all about Jesus's love and grace?

5. Read 2 Corinthians 5:17–20. How does this passage remind you of the responsibility and reinforce the importance of our mission of evangelism?

6. How do Proverbs 11:30 and 1 Corinthians 9:19–23 challenge and encourage you to live your life in order to "win souls"?

CHAPTER 8

Civil Conversations

"We are not responsible to God
for the souls that are saved, but we are responsible
for the gospel that is preached,
and for the way in which we preach it."

CHARLES H. SPURGEON

Recently I received a message on Instagram from someone I didn't know. If you are not familiar with Instagram, it's a popular online social media platform like Facebook or Twitter, but it's photo driven. I like to post inspirational and encouraging quotes from the Bible, photos of people I meet, and snapshots of our church events. I don't follow very many people, but my son used to help me grow my social media accounts and would follow people in hopes they'd follow me back. That's most likely how I started following this guy. And since I don't spend much time browsing through the endless feed of photos from other Instagrammers, he could have been posting photos of aliens every day and I probably never would have noticed.

But one day he sent me the following message:

So umm . . .
I see that you are following me, but I don't understand why?
I'm like a homosexual Satanist and I don't believe in fairy
tales—
*cough, God, *cough
So um yeah . . . unless you want something else from me . . .
I would suggest blocking me.

If you had received this message, what would you have done? How would you have responded? I wanted to say something that wouldn't turn him away. Something that would keep the conversation going. I thought for a moment, started typing, and hit enter.

Why do you consider yourself a Satanist???

I just kind of skipped over the homosexual part and got right to the heart of the matter. And he responded by saying:

Just kidding . . . I'm an atheist.

Then I wrote:

So you are a comedic atheist?

He replied:

I guess . . . haha!

The next day I received this message from the guy:

What do you get from God? What does He do for you?

Wow, did I answer that question with joy! One of the many things I shared was:

> *I feel like I'm never alone. That I am blessed by God and that He has a plan, a direction for my life. I look up at the stars and think there must be a Creator, that none of this is an accident. And I just read the Bible, and it rang true.* ☺

And then I challenged him to *try* to read the Bible. I figured he probably didn't own a Bible, so I wrote:

> *Google "James 1" and read it, and you will see how cool it is—and wise.*

He wrote back:

> *I said . . . I don't read fairy tales*

So then I prayed, "Lord, give me the perfect answer to pique his interest," and I sent him this message:

> *James is a history book! Try just one chapter. What would it hurt? What if it was a vast treasure just at your fingertips? If . . . after reading one chapter, you think it's meaningless, then I'll understand.*

A couple of days went by, and I received a new message in my inbox from him. It read in all caps:

> *BEST READ OF MY LIFE!*

What the World Needs Now

Oftentimes the best way to open the door to sharing Jesus with someone is to begin a civil conversation. This means we maintain a sincere, kind, and respectful tone as we dialogue. It also means praying for the Holy Spirit's guidance about what to say, including when and how to say it.

In the introduction of this book, I observed that as Christians, many of us tend to fall into two different extremes. There are some who don't engage with nonbelievers at all about spiritual matters because they feel afraid, intimidated, or ill-equipped. There are others who do, but it can be in a manner that is obnoxious or argumentative. Let us look to 1 Peter 3:15 as the remedy to both extremes. It says:

> But in your hearts revere Christ as Lord. Always be prepared to give an answer to everyone who asks you to give the reason for the hope that you have. But do this with gentleness and respect.

Our effectiveness for the gospel begins with a reverence for Christ as Lord in our hearts. We are called to always be ready to give an answer to those who ask us the reason why we have hope. And we are to do this with gentleness and respect.

What the world needs now, more than ever before, is for believers to be open, engaging, and available to civil conversations in a culture where people are becoming more and more hostile to Christianity—and to each other. Just look at any comments section of a social media post or news article online. It can be the simplest topic to the most controversial. Doesn't matter. In just about every instance, you will have people who disagree with one another and begin labeling and attacking with no filter. Civil discourse seems to have left the building. And we Christians are just as guilty of this as nonbelievers.

The truth is, we are not going to win anyone or convince anyone of anything with our harsh and obnoxious Facebook posts over petty differences. We are not going to argue anyone into God's kingdom. Instead, let's begin to engage in civil dialogue.

Throughout Scripture, almost every conversion story began with some type of civil conversation. In Acts 8, Philip had a conversation with an Ethiopian who ended up getting baptized. In Acts 10, Peter and a man named Cornelius had a conversation, and the next thing you know, Cornelius and his family surrendered their lives to Jesus Christ. It was in Acts 16:13–14, during a conversation with Paul and his companions, that a woman named Lydia opened her heart to receive Christ as Lord.

Jesus preached and taught the people, but in His one-on-one conversations we see that He would often take on a different approach by conversing and asking questions. One of the best examples of this is recorded in the third chapter of John. A man named Nicodemus had an encounter with Jesus—and his life was forever changed.

Nick at Night

Nicodemus was someone you might meet for the first time and think, *He'll never become a Christian.* The guy had political influence and clout. He represented the status quo. He was wealthy. A guardian of the rules. A keeper of the laws.

Were you raised in (or have you ever been to) a legalistic church? The kind of church that emphasizes "keeping of rules"—lots and lots of rules! Sadly, sometimes even "unwritten" rules are considered biblical.

I had a little of that growing up. I was taught that when Jesus turned water into wine, it was literally Welch's grape juice. And when King David brought home the ark of the covenant, I was told that in the Hebrew text, David wasn't really dancing; he was just nodding his head and tapping his foot.

Nicodemus most likely subscribed to all kinds of unwritten laws as a teacher to Israel. He represents the people who believe that by keeping all the rules they are somehow saved or made righteous. And yet Nicodemus came to Jesus at night because he was probably very intrigued by Him. He wanted to learn more about Him and the things He had been teaching. So Nicodemus said, "Rabbi," which means "teacher," and the conversation began.

> Rabbi, we know that you are a teacher who has come from God. For no one could perform the signs you are doing if God were not with him. (John 3:2)

There are a few things I want to highlight within Jesus and Nicodemus's exchange that will be immensely helpful to you as you share your faith.

Straight to the Point

Jesus was willing to have a civil conversation with Nicodemus, but He also got straight to the point, as we see in the third verse of John 3. It could have been because it was late at night and Jesus was too tired for small talk. But it probably had more to do with Jesus's desire to see Nicodemus saved. He pulled no punches. He did not shy away from this opportunity to converse with one of Israel's most important political and religious leaders.

He said to Nicodemus, "Very truly I tell you, no one can see the kingdom of God unless they are born again."

That's pretty direct. Nicodemus heard this phrase *born again* and he couldn't figure it out; he didn't understand it. So he asked the question heard around the evangelical world: "How can someone be born when they are old? Surely they cannot enter a second time into their mother's womb to be born!" (v. 4).

Jesus answered, and once again, He did not mince words: "Very truly I tell you, no one can enter the kingdom of God unless they are born of water and the Spirit. Flesh gives birth to flesh, but the Spirit gives birth to spirit" (vv. 5–6).

And what He meant by that was that Nicodemus had already been born physically; he needed to be born *spiritually*. Nick at Night still didn't get it, but to be fair, consider where we are in history: Jesus hadn't died on the cross yet, the day of Pentecost was still three years away, and the church hadn't started yet. There were no baptisteries, no communion trays, and no crosses on church buildings. Jesus was speaking somewhat prophetically when He pointed out the truth about being born of the water and the Spirit.

No wonder Nicodemus didn't understand. I'm not sure he was supposed to understand. Even mature Christians today have difficulty understanding this text! And Jesus, like Jack Nicholson in *A Few Good Men*, might have been thinking, *You can't handle the truth!* But he laid everything out directly anyway.

Sometimes when believers are talking with someone who doesn't know Christ, we beat around the bush. We use too many words. We preface or sugarcoat or water down the message. Jesus's civil conversation with Nicodemus teaches us that sometimes we need to get straight to the point. This doesn't mean you should be frantic, rude, or abrupt. Jesus was gentle and at ease as He shared the truth. He is the way, the truth, and the life, after all, so it was probably completely natural for Him!

It may not be as natural to us, but you and I can learn to hone our message. As we practice sharing our testimony and the gospel message (more on this in later chapters), we will learn to cut out all the hemming and hawing and get down to what's most important: the simple story of Christ's transforming love.

The Spirit Is Always Moving

Next Jesus said to Nicodemus, "The wind blows wherever it pleases. You hear its sound, but you cannot tell where it comes from or where it is going. So it is with everyone born of the Spirit" (v. 8).

Nicodemus asked, "How can this be?" (v. 9). The reason he asked this question is because he was convinced that the law was what saved a person.

But since the law cannot save, there was a restlessness in Nicodemus's soul. Despite the fact that he was a "law man"— and had money, fame, power, position, and religion—he was empty inside. He was searching. He didn't know why he was searching. He didn't know why he was feeling what he was feeling.

> As we practice sharing our testimony and the gospel message, we will learn to cut out all the hemming and hawing and get down to what's most important: the simple story of Christ's transforming love.

I imagine Jesus was trying to quiet all the noise in Nicodemus's mind and heart by saying, "Shh! Listen to the sound of the wind. The Holy Spirit of God is drawing you toward something that *can* save."

And here's the best part: even though Nicodemus came searching for Jesus that night, it was actually Jesus via the Holy Spirit who was searching for Nicodemus.

Do you remember the story in the Bible about a man named Zacchaeus who was small in stature? He climbed up a tree to look for Jesus, who was passing through the town of Jericho. Jesus looked up and said to him, "Zacchaeus, come down immediately. I must stay at your house today" (Luke 19:5).

Let me ask you a question: Was Zacchaeus searching for Jesus, or was Jesus searching for Zacchaeus? Even though Zacchaeus was a wealthy tax collector, a "sinner" by everyone else's account, he was valuable to the Lord. Jesus was looking for him and wanted to be a guest in his home. After encountering the Lord, Zacchaeus repented of his sins, vowing to give half of what he owned to the poor and to pay restitution to anyone he cheated in the past.

If there was any doubt that Jesus was in fact looking for Zacchaeus, what the Lord declared next should clear things up: "Today salvation has come to this house, because this man, too, is a son of Abraham. For the Son of Man came to seek and to save the lost" (Luke 19:9–10).

The Spirit of God moved in the heart of a wealthy tax collector to climb that tree in Jericho in order to catch a glimpse of Jesus Christ, the Savior of the world. As we've already discovered, God's Spirit also moved in the heart of Nicodemus to seek out Jesus for the answers to his questions. Behind the scenes, this very moment, the Spirit of God is moving! It blows wherever it wants to. As you approach casual conversations with others, I hope you will take comfort in the fact that God's Spirit is always moving and wooing—even in folks you think would never be saved.

Author and blogger Russell Moore penned this powerful statement:

> The next Billy Graham might be passed out drunk in a fraternity house right now. The next Charles Spurgeon might be making posters for a Gay Pride March right now. The next Mother Teresa might be managing an abortion clinic right now.

But the Spirit of God can turn all that around. And seems to delight to do so.[1]

Don't ever doubt whom God can reach or whom God can save! As Jesus said, the wind blows wherever it pleases. In the poverty-stricken slums of Nairobi and Kolkata, the wind is blowing. In the affluent mansions of Beverly Hills, the wind is blowing. Across the crime-infested ganglands of Chicago, the wind is blowing. Across the decadent playgrounds of the French Riviera, the wind is blowing. In the classrooms and campuses of liberal universities, the wind is blowing. Across the scorching sands of the Middle East where we are seeking to defeat terrorism, the wind is blowing. In little country churches that run sixty people and in the large churches that run six thousand, the wind is blowing.

Right now there are people in your life—and perhaps even folks you have not yet met—who are restless just like Nicodemus. They are wondering what it means to be born again. There is an emptiness in their heart that the law, or self-righteousness, or money, or power, or fame, or relationships, or drugs, or alcohol cannot fill. The Spirit of God could be reaching out to them through you. Let this amazing truth be your confidence as you initiate civil conversations with them about matters of the faith.

Patience—Even When They Don't Understand

After Nicodemus asked, "How can this be?" Jesus continued to talk with him and explained Himself in quite some detail. Even though Nicodemus was a teacher of the law and should have been able to grasp these concepts. Even though, by all appearances, his conversion was nowhere in sight.

And what we learn from Christ's approach and demeanor is that we must be *patient* with others, even when they don't understand.

Jesus patiently took Nicodemus back to a familiar story in Numbers 21 to explain salvation. The people of God were complaining when they should have been rejoicing because God had delivered them from captivity in Egypt and was leading them to the promised land.

They questioned Moses's leadership abilities.

They didn't like the monotonous and dry food. (I like to tell people they were complaining that there was no salsa.)

They began to second-guess leaving a life of slavery in Egypt.

And they began to infect the camp with poisonous words.

So the Lord sent real, live snakes into their midst, to do literally the very thing the people were guilty of doing figuratively: poisoning. Many of the Israelites died. Those who were left realized their sin and went to Moses to repent. They knew they were doomed and beyond hope.

In recounting this story, Jesus reminded Nicodemus how Moses lifted up a bronze snake on a pole and whoever looked upon that snake would live. Just as He did with His "born again" statement earlier, Jesus was juxtaposing the physical with the spiritual. In fact, He told Nicodemus that He was speaking about heavenly things: "Just as Moses lifted up the snake in the wilderness, so the Son of Man must be lifted up, that everyone who believes may have eternal life in him" (John 3:14–15).

> But God has called us to lift up Jesus so that He can draw all people to Him. That is our only job. That is all we have to worry about.

Jesus was patient with Nicodemus as He led him to the truth of the gospel. We are called to do the same in our civil conversations with others. It may look like they don't understand. It may look like they are never going to receive it. But God has called us to lift up Jesus so that He can draw all people to Him (John 12:32). That is our only job. That is all we have to worry about.

At Shepherd Church, we believe lifting up Jesus is so important that it's the name and mission of our television and radio ministry and website—LiftUpJesus.com. Churches, ministries, and colleges worldwide would be a million times better off if we stopped complaining and spent our energies on lifting up Jesus.

More and more every day, our world is becoming so divided and confused. Like the Israelites who had snakes in the midst of their camp, it may seem as though we're all doomed.

Our only hope is Jesus Christ.

In everything we do, in every conversation we have, we believers must be loving, patient, truthful, and above all, lift up Jesus so that the entire world will believe.

It's All God

As I attempt to put myself in Nicodemus's sandals after this fascinating conversation with the Savior of the world, here is what I imagine Nicodemus saying or thinking:

"Jesus, everything that You're saying has completely turned my thought process upside down. Everything I have ever been taught since I was a child is that the *law* is what saves! You come along with these miracles and signs that force me to listen to You. You tell me I have to be born again of water and the Spirit. And that the Son of man must be lifted up."

I imagine him continuing, "Jesus, I'm an educated man, but I need You to simplify this for me. I'm very interested—but I don't understand. I know the Scriptures front to back. I know what the rabbis have taught for thousands of years, but . . . I have no idea what You are saying."

Then, in perhaps the greatest verse in John's entire Gospel,

Jesus really did simplify it all for Nicodemus when He declared: "For God so loved the world that he gave his one and only Son, that whoever believes in him shall not perish but have eternal life" (John 3:16).

People can keep all the laws, but the law can't save. They can be leaders among leaders, but fame and recognition can't save. They can be wealthy, but material possessions cannot save. Only knowing the Son of God—Jesus—can save a person.

Christ went to the cross and died for the sins of the world. All who believe in Him will not perish but have everlasting life! As Jesus spoke amicably with Nicodemus, we can show others through patient, civil conversations that it was all part of God's plan.

God's story.

God's love.

God's Spirit.

God's calling.

God's Son.

God's salvation.

Any time you see people getting saved, lives being changed, miracles and signs, and people moving from darkness to light—it's all God. Anything good you see is because God is at work around the world to redeem mankind before Jesus returns. Unbelievers may not understand this, but we can help them. Today, can you initiate civil conversations about matters of faith with the five people on your list—or maybe even with someone you meet this week? The discussion questions below include a few promptings to help you in. From there, we can move on to the important role that sharing your testimony plays in the evangelism process.

DISCUSSION QUESTIONS

1. How would you have answered an instant message similar to the one I received on Instagram from page 121?

2. How do negative interactions with people damage the ability for others to see God's true love and grace for them? How are words, tones, body language, and actions all related to interactions with people?

3. During your civil conversations and interactions with people you listed after reading chapter 1, how can you better represent Jesus to them?

4. Read John 3:1–21. How does this interaction between Jesus and Nicodemus demonstrate gentleness and kindness during an interaction that could have gotten tense?

5. Read Acts 16:13–14. How did this simple interaction during the normal activities of a day turn around the life of Lydia? What can we learn from this interaction, and how can we apply it to our lives?

6. Invite someone to join you for a cup of coffee, or to your home to be a part of your small group or Bible study this week. Talk with them and get to know them so you have a better perspective on their belief base.

CHAPTER 9

The Power
of a Changed Life

"To every lost soul, Christ says:
Come unto me. To every redeemed soul,
Christ says: Go for me."

UNKNOWN

L et me tell you about a man named Steve who was going down the wrong path in life and almost went to jail before encountering someone who was compelled to tell him about Jesus.

It all started one Friday evening when another man named Robert, who went to Shepherd Church, closed his Jet Ski store in Chatsworth for the night. Before Robert went home, he left one of his Jet Skis outside in front of his shop, secured with a chain and a lock. It had a sign on it that read, "Rent Me."

On Monday morning when Robert returned to his store, the Jet Ski was gone. He asked one of his employees, "Hey, where is the demo unit we kept out front this weekend?"

The employee had noticed it was missing, but he figured

someone else had brought it back inside. Unfortunately, that particular Jet Ski was nowhere to be found and they could only suspect the worst.

The mystery didn't last long, because later that morning a police detective called the shop and said that they had recovered a Jet Ski over the weekend and thought it belonged to Robert's store. The police had stopped a guy in a van for drunk driving, and in the process of taking his information, they found out the van he was driving was a rental that was thirty days past due from being turned in. They also found the stolen Jet Ski.

That afternoon Steve came into Robert's shop and told him that he was the one who took the Jet Ski but that he had intended to bring it back in a few days. Robert also learned that Steve was going through a rough time in his life and was in the process of getting a divorce. The police detective wanted Robert to press charges against Steve, but Robert didn't feel right about it. When he got his Jet Ski back, he was just happy to have his property returned to him.

Robert didn't know what to do, so he called one of our pastors at Shepherd and talked to him about the entire situation for about half an hour. As a result of this conversation, Robert decided to make a deal with Steve. He told him that if he would go to our church every Saturday for three months, then he would not press charges.

The detective was very upset with Robert. He said that the church would not do anything to help Steve. Only jail time would be able to change a man's life. Regardless, Robert made the deal with Steve.

Steve started coming to Shepherd Church. During the first two weeks, he learned about Jesus Christ. He learned about the love, grace, and forgiveness that is found in no one else but Him. On the third week, Robert looked over during the invitation and noticed

Steve stepping forward to give his life to the Lord. Steve was baptized and has been at our church ever since.

Here's a guy who was going through a divorce; he was arrested for driving under the influence; he had a rental van that was thirty days overdue, and he had stolen a Jet Ski. His life seemed like it was over, and yet he met a man who said, "Hey, let me tell you about Jesus Christ and what He has done for you." And the Lord Jesus did the rest.

God stepped in and changed Steve's story. This man's life was going in one direction, and the Lord flipped it 180 degrees. Now Steve has a powerful testimony for the glory of God.

Not Just for You

Think about your life before Christ. Do you remember what it was like? Following your own thoughts and desires. The confusion and fear, or the bondage to sin without peace.

And then one day you surrendered your life to Jesus and became a new person. He came not only to save you but also to change you. Every time you look in that mirror, it's a reminder of that wonderful day you met Christ and of the new person you've become. This week, why not write, "The New Me" on the side of your mirror? What a great way to remember just how God has transformed your life. As 2 Corinthians 5:17 declares, "The old has gone, the new is here!"

> The power of Christ working in your life is what attracts others to, one day, experience their own transformation. Your transformed life speaks of the power of salvation through Jesus.

And while you are reflecting, remember this truth as well: *this transformation was not just for you.* As God is changing you, He is also inviting others to change. The power of Christ working in your life is what attracts others to, one day, experience their own transformation. Your transformed life speaks of the power of salvation through Jesus.

What's Your Story?

Your testimony—the story of how God stepped in and changed you through His Son—is a direct reflection of the undisputable, life-changing power of the gospel. It's one of the most effective tools in our evangelism toolbox. Like Steve, there was an old you before you met the Lord. Maybe you weren't on the brink of divorce and headed to jail for DUI and theft. Maybe the old you was angry, or lustful, or prideful, or deluded by self-righteousness, or prone to lying. But now you have been changed by the goodness and mercy of the Lord. You can glorify God and magnify His message by telling others about how He changed you.

Sharing your testimony is much like being called to take the witness stand in court. Witnesses are bound by law and an oath to tell the truth about what they know and what they've seen. What would happen if the witness took the stand, was asked for his or her testimony, but never opened his or her mouth? I'm not sure the judge would be pleased with that type of response!

The same scenario happens every day in the "court of public opinion" (a.k.a. your everyday world). There comes a time when you will have to do more than wear your favorite Christian T-shirt or a cross necklace, or carry your Bible around at work or school. Sooner or later, you will have to open your mouth and speak. You have to testify. You have to tell what Jesus has done in your life. As 1 Peter 2:9 lovingly explains:

> But you are a chosen people, a royal priesthood, a holy nation, God's special possession, that you may declare the

praises of him who called you out of darkness into his wonderful light.

Let me encourage you to do an exercise that I believe will help you to tell your story. Take out a piece of paper, or you can do so in the study question section at the end of this chapter, and divide it into three sections and label them. These represent three distinctive times of your life:

Section A is your life *before* you became a Christian.
Section B explains *how* you became a Christian.
Section C describes your life *since* meeting Jesus.

Now begin to write out your testimony in each category. (You might need three separate pages, and that's okay.) Section A should be easy because everyone seems to remember how they used to be before they met Jesus! Section B may be a bit more challenging, as not everyone has had a "Damascus Road" experience like Paul did in Acts 9. But every believer should be able to explain when and how they got saved. Section C will detail how God changed you—the areas of your life that God completely rearranged for His glory, and the fruit or evidence of this transformation.

The apostle Paul gave us a great example of this very exercise in Acts 22. Let's look at each section in greater detail now.

Section A

In Acts 22:3–4, we find Paul's "Section A," which is his life before he met Jesus. He wrote,

I am a Jew, born in Tarsus of Cilicia, but brought up in this city. I studied under Gamaliel and was thoroughly

trained in the law of our ancestors. I was just as zealous
for God as any of you are today. I persecuted the followers of this Way to their death, arresting both men and
women and throwing them into prison.

Nice guy, right? Persecuting Christians to their death. And
you thought *your* first section was rough! You might have done
some bad things before you gave your life to Jesus, but I doubt
killing Christians for pleasure was one of them!

Section B

Paul's "Section B," where he explained *how* he got saved, is found
in verses 6 and 7. Here is his testimony:

About noon as I came near Damascus, suddenly a bright
light from heaven flashed around me. I fell to the ground
and heard a voice say to me, "Saul! Saul! Why do you
persecute me?"

As I said before, perhaps your experience wasn't this dra-
matic. Not everyone literally "sees the light," audibly hears the
voice of the Lord, and is blinded for a time like Paul was. But
you need to be able to explain the miraculous moment when you
finally became a believer in Jesus Christ and surrendered your life
over to Him.

Then Paul continued his remarkable story in verses 12
through 16:

A man named Ananias came to see me. He was a devout
observer of the law and highly respected by all the Jews
living there. He stood beside me and said, "Brother Saul,

receive your sight!" And at that very moment I was able to see him.

Then he said: "The God of our ancestors has chosen you to know his will and to see the Righteous One and to hear words from his mouth. You will be his witness to all people of what you have seen and heard. And now what are you waiting for? Get up, be baptized and wash your sins away, calling on his name."

Who was your Ananias in your own salvation story? Who explained the gospel to you, or invited you to church or Bible study? Where were you when you first heard the gospel? Or what was the catalyst—the sermon, event, or prayer—in which God touched your heart? Was it at a youth camp, a Christian retreat, or beside your bed one night as you were crying out to the Lord? Did it happen while you were listening to a sermon on the radio, television, or Internet? Who gave you your first Bible? When and where did you get baptized, and by whom?

Whatever your unique story may be, spend some time writing down your Section B, using these questions as your guide.

Section C

The remainder of Acts 22 is "Section C" of Paul's life. Jesus appeared to him a second time and told him in verse 21, "Go; I will send you far away to the Gentiles." And for the remainder of Paul's life, he was faithful to this calling. His "Section C" was filled with many hardships and challenges, but also with great miracles and teaching. Paul became one of the greatest ministers of the gospel, leading many to salvation and starting influential churches throughout the ancient world.

As you write down your "Section C," ask yourself:

- Who am I now in Christ?
- How is this in contrast to who I was before?
- How has God changed me?
- How is He glorified in me?
- What fruit is displayed in my life? (See Colossians 1:10 and Galatians 5:22–26.)
- How is the work of the gospel evidenced in my life?

Why is this a good exercise? Mainly because I have found that the people who actually write out their story become more confident in telling it to others. Plus, it is always good to recall all that God has done in your life, giving Him all praise and glory. The story of a changed person is a powerful thing.

If you would like to see the most powerful tool of evangelism besides the gospel itself, just look in the mirror. You may appear to be an ordinary person, but you have power inside of you. You are living proof of the good news of Jesus Christ. You have been irreversibly and radically changed by Jesus. It's difficult to dispute the evidence of a transformed life.

It's Only Natural

One day Jesus crossed over a lake, most likely the Sea of Galilee, with crowds of people following Him. He had just rescued a man who had been demon-possessed, casting the torturous spirits into a herd of pigs that then leapt off a cliff and drowned in the lake below (Mark 5:1–20). The only type of rest Jesus received after this gnarly encounter probably was the boat ride across the lake, because it seems that as soon as He reached shore, a desperate father, the leader of a synagogue, approached Him. His daughter was dying. The man, Jairus, begged the Lord to heal his daughter, so Jesus went with him.

But Jesus was divinely sidetracked by a woman with a bleeding disorder who had reached out and touched His cloaked and was healed. During His exchange with her, some people came by and informed Jairus that his daughter had died. "Why bother the teacher anymore?" they asked him (v. 35).

"Overhearing what they said, Jesus told him, 'Don't be afraid; just believe'" (v. 36).

So they went to Jairus's home anyway and were met by crying, wailing, and commotion over the loss of this precious little girl. But Jesus sent them all out of the room and told the child to rise, and she did! The Bible says that everyone was astonished, but "He gave strict orders not to let anyone know about this" (v. 43).

Wait a minute. Jesus just performed an extraordinary miracle and didn't want anyone to say anything about it?

Exactly.

Throughout the Gospels, we see Jesus perform miracles and then, interestingly, instruct people not to tell anyone. In Mark 7:31–36, He healed a man who was deaf and mute: "Jesus commanded [the formerly deaf, mute man and the witnesses] not to tell anyone. But the more he did so, the more they kept talking about it." Another example is in Mark 8:30, when Peter declared that Jesus was the Messiah in front of all the other disciples: "Jesus warned them not to tell anyone about him."

The reason why Jesus kept giving this warning is because He knew that when something good happens to a person, his or her natural inclination is to want everyone to know about it; however, it was not yet time for His identity as the Messiah to be revealed (compare John 2:4 and John 12:23).

Can you imagine if God healed you of stage four cancer, or if He restored your marriage right when the divorce papers were about to be signed, or if He suddenly helped you find a child who was lost? You would tell everybody about it! The words would come out of your mouth like Niagara Falls. Likewise, the best thing that ever happened to you is when Jesus saved you. It's only natural that you would tell people about it. Why would you do that? Because of pure joy and gratitude for what God has done for you—and your desire for others to receive the same!

If you've ever been blessed by Christ, wouldn't you want others to be blessed?

If you've ever been healed by Christ, wouldn't you want others to be healed?

If you've ever been saved by Christ, wouldn't you want others to be saved?

Of course you would! It's only natural!

Recently I said to my congregation, "No minister should ever have to motivate you to share your faith. The reason why is because you were once lost. You were chasing after all kinds of things or you were imprisoned by any number of worldly vices. But Jesus Christ set you free. Naturally, you would want to tell everybody about what He did in your life."

> The best thing that ever happened to you is when Jesus saved you. It's only natural that you would tell people about it.

Simple Truth

One of the greatest, most uncomplicated testimonies of a radically changed life recorded in the Bible is found in John 9. While Jesus and His disciples were walking along the road, He saw a man, blind from birth. Jesus crouched down and made a paste out of some dirt and His spit, then placed it on the man's eyes. Immediately this man could see for the first time in his life.

Everyone praised God—everyone except for the religious leaders of the day. Trying to trap Jesus for breaking the law of working (performing miracles) on the Sabbath, they began questioning this healed man. Not about his sight, but about the One who had performed this miracle. Following much interrogation, this man's final answer was not about a religious tradition or the credibility of his Healer. Instead, he spoke of his new, transformed life:

> Whether he is a sinner or not, I don't know. One thing I do know. I was blind but now I see! (John 9:25)

How simple yet powerful! This man once was blind, but after meeting Jesus, he was able to see. And he is not alone! Every follower of Christ was, at one time, blinded by sin and therefore separated from God. We may not all have a master's degree in ministry or New Testament studies. We may not be able to answer skeptic's questions perfectly. But we can all say, "One thing I do know. I was blind but now I see!"

I think one of the enemy's best tricks is to cause believers to forget how important our testimony is or to fool us into thinking that it's not a big deal. I hope you will always remember the amazing story of how God saved you—and that your testimony is powerful and needs to be shared. As Jesus instructed the demon-possessed man He healed in the Gentile region of Gerasenes where He visited briefly in Luke 8, "'Return home and tell how much God has done for you.' So the man went away and told all over town how much Jesus had done for him" (v. 39).

What Sets Christianity Apart

Showing someone the power of a changed life is very important, but there are many other false religions and ideas that can boast transformation. People report finding peace after doing yoga or practicing Buddhism. Some are cured of addiction through a twelve-step program. Others find purpose in volunteer work or advocating on behalf of an important social cause.

So what makes Christianity different?

The gospel—which we find in God's Word, which details the death, burial, and resurrection of Jesus Christ, God's one and only Son—is what makes Christianity stand apart from any other book or religion or philosophy in the world. No other person in the history of the world has died for your sins and mine. No other person was raised from the grave by Almighty God, conquering death in order to give us new and everlasting life. No other person is now seated at the right hand of God and intercedes for us (Acts 7:55–56; Romans 8:34; Colossians 3:1).

This overwhelming revelation is why it's the responsibility of every believer to learn how to articulate the gospel. To be able to share, from the Bible, what the good news means.

As intimidating as it sounds, even a child can learn the biblical steps to lead someone to salvation. If you're not a prolific communicator, it doesn't matter. With a willing and teachable spirit, God can use you to say the right thing, at the right time, to bring the message of salvation in the right way.

Sharing your testimony is the first step in verbally articulating your faith. The next step is to be able to open the Word of God with joy and confidence and explain the gospel to someone. I'm so excited to begin this part of our journey together, because there is nothing more awesome and satisfying than digging into the treasure of God's Word.

DISCUSSION QUESTIONS

1. Why is hearing a personal testimony so powerful?

2. What are Sections A, B, and C of your personal testimony?

3. Read Acts 26:2–21. In this passage, Paul shares all of his testimony, including some very ugly points of his life. How does this passage encourage you to share your story, regardless of how embarrassing some of your past deeds may have been?

4. How can your life—past, present, and future—be a channel of God's love, Christ's forgiveness, and the Holy Spirit's transformation?

5. Read Mark 5:1–20. This man spent, at most, just a few hours with Jesus before he was sent out to tell his story. How does this convict your inaction and encourage you to share your story regardless of your maturity as a Christian?

CHAPTER 10

Getting God's Word in Your Heart

"If I had to choose between all the disciplines
of the spiritual life, I would choose Bible memorization,
because it is a fundamental way of filling our minds
with what it needs. This book of the law shall not depart
out of your mouth. That's where you need it!
How does it get in your mouth? Memorization."

DR. DALLAS WILLARD [1]

When we have a desire to share Jesus with others and the Word of God is in our heart, the results can be life changing for some. Dusty Frizzell is our youth pastor at Shepherd Church. He is the kind of guy you just want to be around. His demeanor is unfailingly friendly and approachable, and no matter who you are, you feel that he is "for" you—that he actually wants you to soar in your walk with God and in life.

When Dusty was in college, he worked at a sports bar and grill.

One of his coworkers, Joe, was not a Christian. Dusty describes Joe as a typical Generation X guy in his mid-twenties who used a lot of colorful language. Joe lived with his girlfriend and had never stepped foot in a church. But he knew that Dusty went to a Bible college, and every day Joe would ask Dusty questions about God and Jesus, the Bible, Christianity and other religions, and evolution.

One night Joe asked Dusty if he had a Bible that he could borrow; he said he wanted to read something. So Dusty went out to his car, grabbed his Bible, and gave it to Joe. Dusty recommended that Joe start in the book of Matthew. Joe read all twenty-eight chapters of Matthew in one night. And a couple of nights later, he came back to Dusty and said he had been sharing with his girlfriend a lot of the things he and Joe had been discussing. He said his girlfriend told him that when she was in grade school, she had gone to this church camp and had gotten saved. And Joe said, "Dusty, I've never been saved before. What does that mean? What do I do?"

So after closing time that night, Dusty and Joe sat on bar stools there in the restaurant, and Dusty opened up the New Testament and showed Joe what the Bible says about giving one's life to Christ—about being saved. About fifteen to twenty minutes later, Joe shut the Bible and said, "Look, I believe that. I'm ready. What do I need to do to be baptized?"

It was about midnight when Dusty and Joe drove to a lake. And in the middle of a lightning storm, Dusty baptized Joe in the dark waters of that lake.

The first thing Joe asked Dusty after he came out of the water was, "Does the Bible really say that sex outside of marriage is wrong?" Dusty was honest with Joe. He told him about Hebrews 13:1–4 and 1 Corinthians 6:18–20. And so, a few weeks later, Joe moved his girlfriend out of his apartment and into her own apartment. Several months after that, they got married.

Now, obviously, every attempt we make at lifting up Jesus doesn't end like this, but Dusty shares that this experience and some others have taught him this: "People who don't know Christ are not a project or a cause," he said. "They are living, breathing human beings with a soul, and with dreams and pain, just like you and me. Be real and have courage. Take the opportunities that God gives you. Focus on the essentials and be patient. And be prepared to share your life and God's Word concerning salvation."

Almost five years went by after Dusty baptized Joe. By now Dusty was married and in full-time ministry. Joe called him out of the blue, which surprised Dusty because he hadn't spoken to Joe in years. Joe's voice was broken, and he asked to meet with Dusty. Joe shared about his wife, how she had been pregnant and everything had gone normally. Her pregnancy and delivery were great. In the hospital room after their daughter was born, the nurses took the baby, but soon there was panic. They said they needed to take the baby in a helicopter to a hospital in St. Louis, Missouri, immediately. Something was wrong with her heart. Joe rode in the helicopter with his baby, but she died before they arrived.

Joe told Dusty he wanted to pray on the helicopter for God to save his baby, but he didn't pray. He said he had been going to church with his family, but he hadn't prayed in months and that he just wasn't taking his faith seriously. Joe said, "Why should God answer my prayers if I hadn't paid attention to Him at all in months?" He wondered out loud if God had given up on him, if there was any hope in this tragedy, if there were second chances for guys like him.

Dusty said, "Jesus revealed God as Father, and God the Father loves you, Joe. Your daughter's death isn't a punishment to get your attention. That would be astonishingly cruel. I believe God was with you even when you chose not to pray, that He is deeply saddened by the death of your daughter . . . and that He deeply wants to reconnect with you now."

During this terrible tragedy, Joe called Dusty, the man who had opened up the Word and led him to Jesus. You see, Dusty cared so much for Joe's soul all those years prior that he was compelled to show him what the Bible said about salvation. Joe believed and was baptized, and even though he ignored God for a time, the seeds of the gospel that were planted in his heart could not be taken away—and they proved to be a source of wisdom, truth, and comfort when he needed them the most.

The Greatest Gift

The Bible, God's Word, is an unmatched treasure. It is a wealth of wisdom, truth, and personal application. It transforms the heart. The mystery of God's love for mankind is revealed in its pages. It is holy and precious. It is a gift that should never be taken for granted. The Word of God will endure forever (Isaiah 40:8; 1 Peter 1:25), but have you ever imagined what it would be like if your ability to read it or share it was suddenly taken away?

A few years ago, I got up to preach on a Saturday evening and right in the middle of my sermon, my heart started racing. That had never happened to me before, so it was a tad frightening. I got through the two services that night, but Sunday morning I preached at 8:30 a.m. and my heart started racing again. I also got extremely light-headed, as if I was going to faint. This time I actually paused and asked the congregation to pray for me. They did, and I felt okay to finish my message. But afterward I went to my office and closed the door.

I didn't know what to do.

> The Bible, God's Word, is an unmatched treasure. It is a wealth of wisdom, truth, and personal application. It transforms the heart.

Our media team convinced me to show the video recording of my sermon during the next two worship services, and I began the process of trying to figure out what was wrong with my heart.

If you were to experience heart problems, the first thing your general practitioner will do is send you to the plumbing doctor. The plumbing doctor is the person who determines whether your heart is strong. Is the heart enlarged? Are your arteries and veins good? Is everything okay with the plumbing aspect of your heart?

Then they send you to an electrical doctor, and he or she is the one who looks at the electrical impulses that make your heart beat. I was sent to Santa Clarita, a small suburb north of Los Angeles, to a cardiologist named Dr. Sam Kojoglanian. His practice is called "Mender of Hearts." I don't think I thought too much about that because I was scared out of my mind when I walked into his office.

Dr. Sam tried his best to ease my anxiety. He was upbeat and joyful from the moment I met him. He put me on a treadmill, and even though I felt like a giant hamster, I did whatever he asked me to do. He kept encouraging me by saying, "It's going to be okay. Jesus loves you. The Bible is true." He prayed with me, and I just looked at him like, "What kind of doctor are you?"

I learned later that Dr. Sam has a ministry called "Beacon of Hearts" where he travels the world as an evangelist. He is passionate about the Word of God and is eager to share the gospel with anyone who will listen. He's written ten different books, which are more like individual prescriptions that help you get through life. His love for God is as big as his reassuring smile.

Dr. Sam told me I was going to be fine, and he was right. Though I had to take a break from preaching for a few months and was prescribed heart medication, my heart got back in rhythm a few months later. Praise the Lord, I show no more symptoms and feel completely healthy today!

The following year we were so blessed to have Dr. Sam preach at our church's Revival, which is an every-other-year, five-night event with worship music and powerful preaching from guest speakers. Its purpose is to revive hearts for the gospel once again. The night Dr. Sam spoke was electrifying, and he reminded us all that God is not mad at us but is madly in love with us. He kept asking, "What will you do with the gift God has given to you?"

That's a great question.

You see, in the midst of my heart problems, my fear was not the possibility of dying; I know where I'm going when I die, and I am ready to see Jesus. But I remember leaving Dr. Sam's office one day and going up to the parking lot. I began to cry uncontrollably because my fear was that I was never going to get to preach again—that maybe God was saying, "This is it; no more."

This would be devastating to me because my deepest passion in life is to tell as many people about Jesus as I possibly can. The issues with my heart are now under control, but I remember how heartbroken I had been, thinking my days of preaching the gospel may have been over.

Do you see what an incredible gift this is? To have a mind that can form thoughts, and a heart that pumps blood throughout your body to keep you alive, and a mouth that can speak what's on your mind and in your heart? It could all be gone tomorrow. So one of the best ways we can thank the Lord for the gift of health and speech is to tell people about Jesus Christ *today*.

But in order to do that, we need to get the ultimate gift—God's Word—into our heart. We need to cherish the Bible and become biblically literate so that we can easily share the truth with others. In this chapter I want to share with you four ways that you can fall in love with God's Word and become knowledgeable about the Bible, which will help you tremendously in the great work of evangelism!

1. Ask God to Fall in Love

The first step toward getting God's Word in your heart is to ask God to help you fall in love with the Bible. There are many things in this world that can vie for our attention and our affection: social media, television shows, movies, books, games, the Internet, and hobbies. None of these things are inherently bad, but as soon as anything takes up residence on the throne of our heart—meaning we spend more time with it than we do with God—it becomes an idol.

Idolatry in any form is something every believer must watch out for. In 1 Corinthians 10:12, Paul admonished believers that even if they think they are standing firm, they ought to be careful so they don't fall. He warned about various temptations, and then in verse 14, he wrote, "Therefore, my dear friends, flee from idolatry."

Over and over again in the Old Testament, we see well-meaning people who started out strong in their walk with God but easily turned to false gods and idols. Think about Aaron and the golden calf in Exodus 32 or Gideon and the gold ephod in Judges 8. Today we don't think of handcrafted statues to worship, but there are other things we put our trust in or devote an inordinate amount of time to.

We need to repent of this. We need to pray and ask God to forgive us for wasting time on inconsequential or frivolous things. God's Word is what truly matters in the world—the only constant, reliable, and true source.

Every day when we wake up and when we lie down to go to sleep, let us ask the Lord to help us fall in love with His Word. I guarantee you that when you pray this earnest prayer, God will do remarkable things in your heart and incline your heart toward His precious and unfailing truth.

2. Spend Time in the Word

At the same time that you are fervently praying that God would help you fall in love with His Word, it's still essential that you actually spend time reading the Bible each day. Even if you can only commit to reading for ten or fifteen minutes a day, carve out some time to open up the wealth of wisdom and truth in God's Word. You will never, ever regret taking time out of your day to dig into the Word. You have an entire treasure to gain and nothing to lose!

Here is why dedicating time to the Bible each day goes hand in hand with being able to share your faith with others:

Think about your favorite TV show or movie for a moment. You can easily tell others about its premise, plot, and characters, right? Why is that? The reason is because you have devoted *time* to it. You've moved beyond becoming familiar with the show or movie from commercials or word of mouth. Instead, you have seen it with your own eyes and have invested time watching it yourself, and now you *know* the premise, plot, and characters.

I can say without a shadow of a doubt that God wants you to know His Word. When temptations and obstacles come, the Bible, the "sword of the Spirit," as Ephesians 6:17 so aptly describes it, will help you resist and overcome. Proverbs 30:5 asserts that "every word of God is pure; He is a shield to those who put their trust in Him" (NKJV). Second Timothy says,

> All Scripture is given by inspiration of God, and is profitable for doctrine, for reproof, for correction, for instruction in righteousness, that the man of God may be complete, thoroughly equipped for every good work. (3:16–17 NKJV)

Pastor Raul Ries once wrote that we should study God's Word because it is infallible, complete, totally authoritative, sufficient for all our needs, and accomplishes what it promises.[2] And if that weren't enough, we should become students of the Bible because people who know His Word are able to share His Word with others. Without a doubt, spending time in God's Word gets God's Word into your heart.

3. Memorize Scripture

If for some reason you did not or could not have your Bible anymore, what Scriptures are engraved on your mind and heart that could bring you comfort? Dear friend, if you are not engaging in the critical exercise of memorizing Scripture, I want to encourage you to start today! Please don't sell yourself short by saying you're not the memorizing type. The human brain is amazing—yours included! We are so blessed to be able to learn new information, ideas, and methods each and every day.

Did you know that information is transferred from your short-term memory to long-term memory through the hippocampus in your brain? It doesn't matter who you are, what you do for a living, what your IQ is, whether or not you've gone to college. Every brain is capable of this fascinating process, which takes place constantly when you learn something new. Here is what I learned recently from a McGill University article on the subject:

> All of the pieces of information decoded in the various sensory areas of the cortex converge in the hippocampus, which then sends them back where they came from. The hippocampus is a bit like a sorting [center] where these new sensations are compared with previously recorded

ones. The hippocampus also creates associations among an object's various properties.

When we remember new facts by repeating them or by employing various mnemonic devices, we are actually passing them through the hippocampus several times. The hippocampus keeps strengthening the associations among these new elements until, after a while, it no longer needs to do so. The cortex will have learned to associate these various properties itself to reconstruct what we call a memory.[3]

Do you know what this means? It means that exercising your memory actually strengthens it! And one way to do so is by repetition. If you repeat important Scriptures over and over to yourself, they will be stored in your long-term memory just like the lyrics of your favorite songs or lines from your favorite movies. You can pull them from your brainy Rolodex at any time when you are sharing your faith with someone, thereby backing up your testimony and your beliefs with the Word of God.

You probably already know this one by heart. It's a verse we discussed when talking about Jesus's interaction with Nicodemus, and it's also one that is repeated over and over again from the time we are little kids, so it has been stored in most of our long-term memories:

> For God so loved the world that he gave his one and only Son, that whoever believes in him shall not perish but have eternal life. (John 3:16)

That is a very good, foundational verse to know by heart, and you probably already do! You may already know this one as well:

Jesus answered, "I am the way and the truth and the life. No one comes to the Father except through me." (John 14:6)

Now it's time to build on your knowledge by memorizing several other scriptures that are essential to sharing your faith. At the back of this book there are some verses—just ten—that we've designed for you to cut out and place in your home, office, or car to help you memorize them. These scriptures are very helpful in explaining our need for salvation and leading someone to put his or her trust in Jesus Christ. You may recognize a few that come from "Romans Road," which is a method to share the gospel with someone using several powerful verses from the book of Romans.[4]

> If you repeat important Scriptures over and over to yourself, they will be stored in your long-term memory just like the lyrics of your favorite songs or lines from your favorite movies.

You can also find the official book page for *Compelled* on Facebook, Instagram, and Twitter. It would be helpful to follow any or all of these social media pages as we will be posting verses and other inspirational tips and tools weekly.

Please commit to reading these evangelistic scriptures and repeating them to yourself for just five to ten minutes a day. Make it a priority. There is nothing more precious or important than the life-changing Word of God. I promise you, if you do this, your confidence in sharing the gospel will skyrocket!

4. Have a Plan Wherever You Go

Once you've committed to memory these key Bible verses that explain salvation, you might begin to wonder how you would even broach the topic of Christianity with someone. God's Word is in your heart, so you'll be grounded in the Bible whatever you say! But it's good to have a plan in place to initiate important spiritual conversations.

One great way is to ask someone what they believe about the soul and the afterlife. You can ask someone what they believe happens after we die. You can also ask if they believe in God and what they believe about where we came from. After you've listened and perhaps asked some good follow-up questions such as, "Why have you come to this conclusion?" usually someone will reciprocate interest in your beliefs and ask you similar questions. Then, with gentleness and respect, you can open up your Bible and share the gospel or the scriptures you have memorized.

You can do this no matter where you are in the world. I've traveled extensively throughout my life, and usually when someone in a foreign country realizes I'm from America, they immediately want to talk to me. Maybe it's because I'm really tall, bald, and kind of stand out in a crowd. But it probably has more to do with the fact that people in many parts of the globe are fascinated with American freedom and culture. If you've done any travel, perhaps you've had the same experience or noticed the same thing.

No matter where I've visited, I have found an easy way to open the door to talking to someone about my faith. Whether it's a cab driver, a server at a restaurant, a tour guide, or the concierge at your hotel, just ask, "What is the major religion here?" Wherever you go, you can ask that simple question. And they'll tell you. Nine times out of ten, the person you're asking practices that religion.

So then you ask them, "What does that religion teach about the afterlife? If I become a Buddhist or a Muslim or a Hindu, what do I have to do to get into heaven?"

It's very possible that no one has ever asked them that question. They might hem and haw for a little bit, but after a while, they'll usually say, "Do these several things," or "Stay away from these things."

There is your open door.

That is when you can share the truth from God's Word. It doesn't matter if you're in your city or a city on the other side of the world, you are now equipped to find that open door and clearly tell someone about the good news of Jesus Christ!

One day, probably very soon, someone you know or someone you meet will have questions about life. They might be searching or have doubts or are going through a difficult time. They may notice something different about you and wonder why that is.

This is the moment of truth. Actually, it's the moment for *the Truth* to come to light—through you! I cannot stress enough how important it is for you to know what the Bible says about salvation. Knowing how the Bible leads a person to a saving knowledge of the truth will equip you and give you more confidence than you ever thought possible. "So then faith *comes* by hearing, and hearing by the word of God" (Romans 10:17 NKJV).

Sometimes it's as easy as dropping a card in the mail or making a phone call to one or all of the people on your list. Then take the next step. Ask them, "Hey, can I meet you for coffee?" Or, "How about a round of golf this week?" That's about four hours (or six hours if you play with me) of uninterrupted time. Then tell them about the greatest book you've ever read, the Bible, and what it says about how we can spend eternity with God.

Share the scriptures you've learned throughout this chapter and keep reading the Word. When you read the Bible over and over again, two things will happen. First, you will fall in love with God's Word. Second, it will become inextricably stored in your heart and your long-term memory—ready to share with anyone at a moment's notice.

Your responsibility as a believer in Christ is simply to be His messenger. It's not up to you to see that person get saved on the spot. That may happen sometimes, and praise God when it does! But more than likely the process of evangelism will take place over many conversations, as we will see in the next chapter.

DISCUSSION QUESTIONS

1. What do you find most difficult about memorizing Scripture?

2. Read John 14:26. According to this verse, what is one of the Holy Spirit's jobs? What is this verse implying about the memorization of Scripture? In other words, how are we to know what the Spirit is reminding us of if we are not reading the Bible?

3. Why is Scripture memorization so important for evangelism? How does God use memorized Scripture during your conversations with people? (See Isaiah 55:11 and Hebrews 4:12.)

4. Write about a time when God brought some verses to your mind during an interaction with someone who did not yet know Christ. What verses were they, and how did the other person respond?

5. Read Matthew 4:1–11. How did Jesus combat Satan while being tempted? How does this passage encourage you to memorize Scripture?

CHAPTER 11

The Patient Process
of Planting

"The way you store up treasure in heaven
is by investing in getting people there."

RICK WARREN

Back before my knees started hurting, I used to enjoy spending Monday nights playing in the adult men's basketball league in our sports ministry at Shepherd Church. Not only was it a fun way to get some exercise, but it was also a great opportunity to introduce people to Jesus through the common bond of sports. That's the mission of our church's sports ministry, Shepherd Sports.

One night a young man named Grayson Boucher showed up to play.

If you were to see Grayson on the street and didn't know who he was, you probably wouldn't guess that he's a world-famous "streetball" basketball player. He's a five-foot-ten white guy with an unassuming, laid-back disposition. He's also the star of the Spider-Man basketball videos that have garnered a combined total of more than 150 million views on YouTube.

But while you might be fooled by his appearance, Grayson—best known as "The Professor" from the highly stylized AND1 Mixtape and Ball Up Tours—would quickly wow you with his extraordinary skills once the basketball touched his hands.

The AND1 Mixtape Tour was the most popular movement in professional basketball ever outside of the NBA. It had a street style that was very flashy with a high skill level and some of the most explosive athletes. Grayson, whose father introduced him to basketball when he was two years old, became a fan of the tour in his teenage years.

In the summer after Grayson's freshman year in college, AND1 hosted a nationwide contest for unknown talent to compete for a contract with the company and a spot on the team. One of their tryouts was held in Portland, Oregon, which was a one-hour drive north of Grayson's hometown. Grayson knew he had to go for it.

Up until this point in time, Grayson had endured many setbacks in the pursuit of his passion for basketball. Many coaches wouldn't give him a chance because he was small in size. On his freshmen team high school roster, he was listed at four foot eleven and eighty-five pounds. He didn't play varsity basketball until his senior year in high school. But with a lot of hard work and his parents' support and encouragement, Grayson was ready when his moment arrived.

At the AND1 tryout, the crowd went wild when he crossed over his opponents a few times and threw a couple of no-look passes. Grayson made it to the final two players in the tryout and was selected to compete in the main event against the AND1 team that night in the NBA Portland Trail Blazers' arena. After a solid performance and a standing ovation from the crowd, AND1 crowned him the winner.

That summer in 2003 was life changing for Grayson. He

traveled the world with AND1 until 2009. He was on television several times a week, met people he never thought he would meet, and was recognized everywhere he went. Plus, he was doing what he loved—and making more money than he knew what to do with.

"Honestly, during those years, I rarely took time to think about bigger questions of life such as, 'What is my true purpose?'" Grayson later shared with me. "Or, 'What happens when we die?' Or, 'What do I believe in spiritually?' It wasn't until discomfort set in that I could really focus on these matters."

After AND1, Grayson immediately began making way less money. The market wasn't demanding streetball like it had in past years, so there were fewer opportunities to play in events. His future was uncertain, and he was barely making rent each month. Finally, he had to drain his entire savings account just to stay above water.

"It was a lonely time," he said.

Then Grayson's friend Demetrius—who would later create a new streetball company called Ball Up—brought him to our basketball gym at Shepherd. Demetrius introduced Grayson to me, our sports ministry pastor, Josh Merrill, and a leader named Chris Ray.

Chris clicked with Grayson right away and often invited him to be his guest at church. Grayson would always decline or make up an excuse. Even though he had a lot of downtime at that point in his life, he said he had no ambition to go to church. He didn't see the need or reason to go.

One night after a game, I asked Grayson to stay and talk with me in my office. He agreed, later telling me that because I seemed like a nice guy and a supporter of his basketball career he thought, *Why not?*

"Do you believe in God, Grayson?" I asked him.

Grayson said yes, but shared years later that he had said it just to appease me. (Though Grayson attended a small Christian school in his youth, he said what he learned about God went in one ear and out the other because he was so consumed with basketball.) I told Grayson he was always welcome at Shepherd, gave him several books to read, and prayed for him.

"I thought that was real generous," Grayson said, looking back. "But sadly, when I got home I remember throwing the books in a storage compartment in my closet and never giving them a second look."

But God's pursuit of Grayson did not end there.

A year later, Chris Ray invited Grayson to church for the umpteenth time and Grayson finally said yes. He found church intriguing and went a few more times before he began attending Shepherd's college-age service. He admits today that he was more of a spectator but began to feel God's presence. He would read the Bible now and then and examine what he believed theologically.

In early 2011, Grayson signed with Ball Up, the basketball tour Grayson's friend Demetrius founded. He was traveling the world again, making money, greeting fans, and being on TV. But seeds of truth continued to get planted in his heart—even when he would soon be confronted by sudden tragedy.

One of his closest friends was his teammate Troy Jackson, better known as Escalade. Escalade was six foot nine, weighed about four hundred pounds, and was the brother of former NBA star Mark Jackson. When Escalade died suddenly of a heart attack, it was the biggest hit Grayson had ever taken emotionally. Grayson traveled to New York for Escalade's funeral. To his surprise, Mark Jackson was there preaching.

"Listening to Mark was really inspiring," Grayson said. "I was at a place in my life where I was empty and defeated. Basketball didn't seem like it was that important at the time. Not too much did. At the end of the service when Mark gave an altar call, I went forward and gave my life to Christ. I figured it was time, and that it would be foolish not to."

Grayson continued to go to Shepherd when he got back from New York. By researching the Word and everything else he could get his hands on, he came to a place where he was convinced that Jesus really was the Son of God. Soon after, Grayson was baptized in the Pacific Ocean.

"God used numerous people at Shepherd, Mark Jackson, and many more faithful people to get me to that point," Grayson shared. "Since then, I have a completely new perspective on life. I believe that through everything, God has put me right where He wants me to be—with a large platform, using the gift He gave me in basketball to bring Him glory. He freed me from many things and gave me a whole new way of life."

Planting Seeds

Grayson's journey to accepting Jesus Christ is excellent proof of a very important principle in evangelism: oftentimes it takes multiple people sharing the truth of the gospel—and multiple times of follow-up—before someone gets saved.

Evangelism is a process.

No one should ever feel the pressure is all on him or her to lead a person to Christ. God may use you today to share the gospel with a loved one or an acquaintance. He may use you again through another conversation down the road. He may use someone else a week, a month, or a year later.

Do you realize that any time you share your faith with someone, you're probably not the first one to do so? And you may not be the last. Not all people get saved the first time they are introduced to the gospel. It might take two, three, four, or more times before someone says yes to Jesus.

Think about the last person you shared Christ with. You could have been the seventh . . . or the third . . . or the tenth person to plant the seeds of the gospel in his or her life. Or maybe you were his or her very first encounter with the message of salvation. Whatever the case, never become discouraged. Keep reminding yourself that God put you in this person's path to share Christ today, regardless if it's the first time or the umpteenth time. And more importantly, if that person doesn't respond, then God has you setting him or her up for someone else who will "reap the harvest."

> Not all people get saved the first time they are introduced to the gospel. It might take two, three, four, or more times before someone says yes to Jesus.

Remember: God's plan is at work, and you are a part of that plan!

Paul was telling the church at Corinth this same principle when he said in 1 Corinthians 3:6, "I planted the seed, Apollos watered it, but God has been making it grow."

Before anyone can see or receive any type of harvest, that person must first be willing to plant the seed. Beautiful gardens don't pop up overnight by themselves. Someone planted. It's a thankless job, but someone has to do it.

Southern California is home to one of the most famous amusement parks in the world: Disneyland. Millions of people from around the world visit each year for the nostalgia and entertainment that only the Magic Kingdom can offer. During the park's operation hours, thousands of employees—from restaurant workers to maintenance crews—work hard to ensure their guests' experience is one they will remember for a lifetime. It's often been said that not only is the Magic Kingdom "the happiest place on earth," it is also the cleanest. But what people do not see is all the work that goes on after the park closes.

Just about as many people work during the night as when the park is open. One of the most important evening responsibilities belongs to the landscape and garden crews. They comb the entire park, replanting and watering thousands of flowers every night. The park guests never see their hard work but are taken aback by the fruit of their labor—all the beautiful landscaping—the next morning when the park opens.[1]

Any time you share your faith, you could be prepping the soil, weeding, planting, or reaping the harvest. You are doing good work—the results of which you may never get to see. No matter which piece of the puzzle you are, the Bible says you will be rewarded according to your labor (1 Corinthians 3:8). And in the end, God brings the increase, the kingdom of God is expanded, and God gets all the glory!

As we talked about in previous chapters, we should always keep in mind that the Holy Spirit is working around the world—this very moment. Even as you are reading these words, He's located someone who is ready and is preparing them to receive the message of salvation. At the exact same time, He's preparing you and me for the divine purpose of delivering the message.

Wherever you go, be sensitive to the Holy Spirit tugging on your heart. You might feel the leading to invite someone to church or share what God has done in your life. Go for it! Surrender and obey! You have no idea what has been happening in that person's life and how the Holy Spirit has prepared him or her to receive the message that you are going to give!

And if you are rejected and the person acts as if he or she doesn't want anything to do with Jesus, don't be discouraged. You may have just been the planter or the waterer in that person's life that day. I love how Chris never gave up asking Grayson to come to church with him, even though Grayson said no a dozen times. Then God used me to plant another seed. Then our college pastor. And God used Pastor Mark Jackson to finally seal the deal.

Don't be afraid to be the third, seventh, tenth, or the fortieth person in that chain!

No Off-Season

The key to being involved in the seed-planting process is preparation. Always being ready. The most excellent athletes in the world have this principle down pat.

Every sport has an off-season. This is the time when players who have been enduring a long, exhausting season take a break to relax and rejuvenate. All sports have these designated periods of rest. The best competitors will take a few weeks to allow their bodies to recuperate, but then they'll use the rest of the time to *prepare* for the next season.

They train.

They lift weights.

They run.

They go through drills.

They push their bodies to the limit so that they'll not only be ready for the next season but will also be *better* than the previous season.

The Bible clearly states that there is no off-season for an ambassador of God. Paul wrote to his protégé, Timothy, "I give you this charge: Preach the Word; be prepared in season and out of season; correct, rebuke and encourage—with great patience and careful instruction" (2 Timothy 4:1–2).

Notice this wasn't a casual suggestion, but a *charge*. A strong command for all believers—not just pastors—to be ready to preach the Word anytime, anywhere, to anyone. When it's convenient, and when it's not. When it's easily accepted, and when it is adamantly rejected. Our circumstances, situations, or surroundings do not alter the charge.

The mandate is still the same—no matter if you're in Southern California or Seattle, Mexico City or Bangladesh, South Africa or any other region of the world: preach the Word!

God's Word is precious. It is the everlasting, unchanging Truth. We as believers have been given the awesome responsibility to become stewards of the Word of God. It is our duty and spiritual obligation. Now is the time to preach the gospel . . . more than ever before. It is exciting to anticipate Jesus's return to this earth—but until that happens, there are specific mandates God has made clear to every Christian:

Receive the Word. Be faithful with the Word. And preach the Word as often as you can.

Czarek's Story

Do you remember Jenn and Vance, the couple I told you about in chapter 1 who are doing ministry in Poland? Well, they began a Bible study in their home, and at first only a few people attended. After a while, their Bible study grew. Vance began a discipleship program for the men who wanted to be discipled, and Jenn did the same for the women.

> Receive the Word.
> Be faithful with
> the Word. And preach
> the Word as often
> as you can.

One day Ewa (pronounced just like "Eva"), one of the women Jenn had been discipling, told Jenn about her coworker named Czarek (pronounced "Char-eck"). When Czarek first found out that Ewa was a Christian, he began to tease her about her faith. Ewa would preach the gospel and he would try to disprove her beliefs. She endured his mockery with grace and patience, but it became very difficult. This went on for about four months. Ewa didn't know how much longer she would be able to take it. Czarek especially did not like it when Ewa told him that we are saved by grace and not by works.

Then Czarek began to ask her questions. Difficult questions. Ewa tried her best to answer as many as she could, and then she told Czarek, "I can't evangelize you anymore, but I can take you to this American family and they will talk to you." After a while, Czarek agreed.

So Czarek went to Vance and Jennifer's house. They told him their story, and he told them his. Czarek grew up Catholic but admittedly did not have a relationship with God. He thought he had faith, but when Ewa told him he was not saved by works, that touched him very deeply so he began to search these things on his own. When he was young, Czarek started training in martial arts and progressed very quickly. As he got older, he met a lot of people through Mixed Martial Arts (MMA) who showed him what adrenaline and the dark world of fighting really looked like. He became addicted to drugs, women, and fights, and his life started to go downhill. Then he got a job at a great company, and it was there that he met Ewa for the first time.

Czarek came to Vance and Jennifer's house with a list of questions. Questions like, "Is God good?" "How do we know the Bible is true?" and questions about the Catholic church. Vance and Jenn spent all evening answering them.

At some point in the evening, Czarek had to pause because he felt a strange feeling throughout his body and in his chest. He didn't know what it was but said it felt warm and peaceful.

"What is that?" Czarek asked.

Vance and Jennifer tried hard to stifle giggles because here was this tough MMA guy sitting in front of them. On top of that, Czarek had ties to the mob, so naturally they did not want to upset him or cause him to think they were laughing at him. But Vance and Jenn knew the Holy Spirit was moving and working through the truth of God's Word, and it was exciting to see that unfold before their very eyes.

"What's happening to me?" he asked them again.

"It's the Holy Spirit," Vance answered.

A short while later, Czarek surrendered to Christ as his Lord and Savior. A short while after this commitment, he was called to testify for the mob in a court case and was supposed to tell one "small" lie. The case had to do with ninety people. But with his newfound faith and what he was learning about God's Word, Czarek couldn't lie. He had to go before the main leaders of the mob and explain why. They split into two groups, and one wanted to hear him out. God moved in their hearts to have mercy on Czarek. There are still people who are angry with Czarek today for not telling that lie, but his burden is to obey God before man.

And guess what? Czarek and Ewa are now married. They have become leaders within the same church-planting organization that Vance and Jenn are a part of. Recently, Czarek spent several weeks leading three men, who were unbelievers, through a Bible study. All three accepted the gospel, and Czarek is discipling them!

When Others Question

Since evangelism is a process that often requires follow-up, you should know that there is a real possibility people may express doubts. Like Czarek, they may have questions, and you may not have the answers to those questions right then and there. That's okay!

One of the most encouraging sentences you need to add to

your vocabulary is this: "I don't know, but let me try to find out for you!"

Then go home and open your Bible. Pray and ask God to give you understanding. Research the question online from reputable Christian websites. Talk to a pastor at your church. Order a book online that may address the issue. (*Evidence That Demands a Verdict* by Josh McDowell and *Dinner with Skeptics* by Jeff Vines are both excellent books.) When you feel you have discovered an adequate answer, call your friend and invite them out for coffee. Share your findings with them.

This may lead to more questions. Pray and ask for discernment. If the person is genuinely interested in what you believe, think of the time you're spending on these conversations as an investment in their eternity. It's also a good thing for you to be learning constantly in order to effectively defend the hope you have in Jesus. William Lane Craig once wrote,

> If Christians could be trained to provide solid evidence for what they believe and good answers to unbelievers' questions and objections, then the perception of Christians would slowly change. Christians would be seen as thoughtful people to be taken seriously rather than as emotional fanatics or buffoons. The gospel would be a real alternative for people to embrace.[2]

Now, there are also times when skeptics will try to bait you into a foolish argument or flat out reject you. Let's talk about that likely scenario now.

DISCUSSION QUESTIONS

1. How does Grayson's testimony on page 166 encourage you to plant seeds of truth in others' lives and to be patient with them?

2. As you think back on your life, what individuals planted seeds during your journey to knowing God? What kind of relationship did you have with them? How did they plant those seeds?

3. Describe how important you think those individual seeds were to your coming to Christ. What are some of the possibilities that could have happened to you if those seeds had not been planted?

4. What kind of relationship do you need to have with people in order to plant seeds in their lives? Why do you think having a relationship with people is so important?

5. What is the difference between planting and watering seeds? What relationships are you more likely to plant and which ones are you more likely to water?

6. Read Matthew 13:1–23. What was the farmer's method for planting seeds, and what was the outcome? Based on this passage, how specific do we need to be when we are planting seeds?

CHAPTER 12

The Reality of Rejection

"If we are devoted to the cause of humanity,
we shall soon be crushed and broken-hearted,
for we shall often meet with more ingratitude
from men than we would from a dog;
but if our motive is love to God, no ingratitude
can hinder us from serving our fellow men."

OSWALD CHAMBERS

In one of the towns where I preached, there was a man I had spoken to many times about the gospel. His wife attended my church and wanted so badly for her husband to join her. She would invite me over to the house to talk to him. He was retired and had plenty of time on his hands. I would invite him to church, and though he was always cordial with me, he would respond to every invitation by saying, "Well, I would, but I gotta go fishing, Preacher. Maybe one day I'll come over and visit."

That was always his response. He never came to visit on a Sunday. Not once.

Every time we had a guest preacher at church, I'd tell them, "Hey, we gotta go see this one guy." I tried to get everyone I knew to work on him! It didn't matter if I was the one who ultimately led him to Jesus or if it was someone else—I just had to try one more time to get him saved. But each time he would say, "I gotta go fishing."

One night a nasty storm came and tore through the area. When it was over, I checked the news, and the leading story concerned a man who had capsized in his boat while fishing during the storm and drowned. I had a sinking feeling in my stomach. Could it be the same man I had grown to care about during my many visits to his home? When they named the man in the report, my fears became reality. It was the same man who had refused to come to church all those years.

I was devastated. The news came like a punch to the gut. There's nothing like the sadness you feel when you're truly burdened for someone and when you're trying to win them over to the Lord and then suddenly the opportunity evaporates.

It breaks your heart.

But it also has the power to light a fire in your bones.

It builds in you a greater resolve for the next person. As much as you might think, it won't cause you to shrink back in fear if you don't allow it to. In fact, the exact opposite can happen. It will kindle in you an even greater desire to reach the world.

No One Likes Rejection

The truth is there isn't one person on the planet who likes to face rejection. It's painful. It hurts. As much as many of us can remember the stories of our victories and our triumphs, the stories of our failures and rejections are often more vivid. Rejection can pierce even the thickest of hides and leave behind a painful and venomous memory that will linger for days, weeks, or even years.

I recently read about a 2014 study from the University of British Columbia that surprised me. Their study centered around people who were ignored at their place of employment; men and women who were given the cold shoulder by their fellow coworkers. According to their study, people who were ignored at work suffered more mental and emotional abuse than people who were outright harassed or bullied. Imagine that! People at work would rather be made fun of or picked on than ignored entirely.[1]

What if we applied these same findings to preaching the gospel? It would mean that we have the emotional fortitude to endure arguments, mockery, and jokes that may result if we choose to lift up Jesus with our words and actions among our peers. What should bother us much more is to be seen as another silent Christian who won't engage about matters of faith and to be ignored altogether.

Rejection is a different monster. In fact, according to neuroscientist Matthew D. Lieberman, the pain we feel when we are rejected is the same as physical pain. After looking at scans of the human brain during tests where the subjects were "rejected" and where subjects experience real, physical pain, he said, "You wouldn't have been able to tell the difference." The scans looked identical.[2]

Doesn't that make sense? Rejection hurts! No wonder we go to such lengths to avoid it. In fact, it may be the one wall that stands in your way to delivering the gospel to that one person who needs to hear it. You're afraid that they're going to reject you. You're afraid that you'll lose a friendship and that they'll never talk to you again. And it is most likely that fear of rejection that prevents you from sharing the truth with them, even though it's the most important thing in the entire world.

Jesus addressed this very real possibility when he said in Luke 10:16, "Whoever listens to you listens to me; whoever rejects you rejects me; but whoever rejects me rejects him who sent me."

In the end, it's not you that they're rejecting—it's Jesus. And they're rejecting God the Father, the One who sent Jesus!

Consider that every time you hear no when you present the gospel, it isn't said to you. It is spoken to the One who sent you.

Remember, you're the ambassador. Your job is to bring the message on behalf of another; in this case the God of the entire universe.

> All of the prophets—Isaiah, Jeremiah, Ezekiel, Amos, and others—were rejected by the very people they had come to help.

You cannot take it personally when you hear that "no" because, trust me, you're going to hear it more than you'd like. We have to get over ourselves. It's not about us but about the One who gave us the greatest mission in the world. Rejection is just par for the course. Ask any of the faithful messengers in the Bible, and I'm sure they'd agree.

Occupational Hazards

At one point or another, every single character in Scripture who stood on God's behalf faced rejection. For instance, do you know what happened when Joseph told his brothers about a dream he had received from God? Those ten brothers of his became enraged with jealously and not only rejected him but sold him into slavery![3]

After Moses led the people of Israel to freedom and into the wilderness, they rejected his message and his leadership and turned their hearts back to Egypt (Acts 7:39–41).

All of the prophets—Isaiah, Jeremiah, Ezekiel, Amos, and others—were rejected by the very people they had come to help

(Daniel 9:6). By accepting God's calling, every person realized the occupational hazard of rejection.

Even Jesus, the Son of God and the Savior of the world, was rejected. In fact, His rejection was actually promised before He was born! One of the many prophecies made about Him in the Old Testament was that He would be rejected. Check out this prophecy from Isaiah 53:3, which was written seven hundred years before Jesus was born in Bethlehem:

He was despised and rejected by mankind,
> a man of suffering, and familiar with pain.
Like one from whom people hide their faces
> he was despised, and we held him in low esteem.

Psalm 118:22–23 is another eye-opening prophecy that was written about Jesus about three hundred and fifty years before Isaiah even took up a pen! It reads:

The stone the builders rejected
> has become the capstone;
the LORD has done this,
> and it is marvelous in our eyes.

The fulfillment of this prophecy shows up repeatedly in the New Testament, highlighting the fact that Jesus—the cornerstone upon which our faith and salvation are built—was rejected. And by the builders, no less! Jesus would be rejected by the very people He had come to save, and that is precisely what came to pass.

The problem of rejection was so prevalent in the Bible that Jesus even told a parable about it in Luke chapter 14 about a man who prepared a great banquet and invited many guests. Now, the banquet was a symbol. It stood for the Marriage Supper of the Lamb, which is being prepared in heaven for those who are saved. It was a metaphor for eternity with God.

In the parable, the table had been set. The meal was prepared. And then the call went out: "Come, for everything is now ready" (v. 17).

It seems fairly simple, doesn't it? It was basically a big party. All anyone had to do was show up. After all, who would say no to free food?! But the Bible goes on to say that no one who was invited accepted the invitation! Not a single person. Instead, they offered up pathetic excuses why they could not attend.

The first guy said, "I have just bought a field, and I must go and see it" (v. 18).

How does that even make sense? Who buys a piece of property without looking at it first? Wouldn't you have seen your piece of real estate before you bought it? Not to mention this wasn't some $4 million mansion on prime real estate. It was a field. A simple, boring field. What was there to see?

The second excuse the man received wasn't any better: "I have just bought five yolk of oxen, and I'm on my way to try them out" (v. 19).

The same question arises! Wouldn't you have tried them out before you bought them?

It's like the person today who says, "I bought a boat, and I need to take it out this weekend to make sure it runs." That's ridiculous.

As if it couldn't get any worse, look at the final excuse: "I just got married, so I can't come" (v. 20). My response to that would be, "Well, then bring your wife! RSVP for two! In fact, everyone else declined the invitation, so there's room for your entire family if you'd like!"

At the end of the day, every person offered petty justifications and inadequate reasons not to come and eat from the Bread of Life. (Imagine how it would feel to invite all those people and be rejected by every single one.) And human nature has not changed. People today still give the most unbelievable excuses for refusing to believe the gospel or even coming to church. With every excuse, they are rejecting the Messenger who offers them eternal life.

If anything, take solace from the fact that this is nothing new. People have been rejecting God ever since the Garden of Eden, and they'll continue to do so until Jesus returns and sets all things right. Until then, we have to learn how to face rejection and handle it with grace.

I Like Your Christ, But . . .

Of all the reasons someone can give for not giving their life to Jesus, here's one I'm sure you've heard: "The church is full of hypocrites."

The word *hypocrite* comes from the Greek word *hypokrites,* which means "I play the part."[4] So hypocrisy, in its simplest form, is pretending to be something you are not. Actually, before they were called actors, people who performed in theaters were called hypocrites because they played a part that was not really themselves. Thus, two actors' masks—one happy face and one sad— were displayed in every theater, hanging on each side of the curtains, to remind the audience what they were about to see was only a portrayal. Or, in other words, just an act.

The same can be said for many professing Christians today. They "play a part" that is not really them, hiding behind the mask of Christianity while never living a truly transformed life. Even though they may get away with their act for some time, it is a dangerous lifestyle that has a tragic ending—not only for them, but also to those who are watching.

During the great independence movement in India, there was no greater political or spiritual leader than Mahatma Gandhi. In this era of history, he was a man of unprecedented power and influence. One of his main missions in life was to bring social justice and spiritual freedom to a destroyed nation. What better way to accomplish this feat than through the power of Jesus Christ, right? The mission field lay wide open for the gospel, but there was a superseding concern. Gandhi described it in these haunting words: "I like your Christ; I do not like your Christians. Your Christians are so unlike your Christ."[5]

Gandhi died in 1948, which means that many Christians were "playing the part" back then. To him, the materialism and arrogance displayed in Christian nations contradicted Jesus's teachings.[6] And he wasn't finished. Gandhi also made this statement: "If Christians would really live according to the teachings of Christ, as found in the Bible, all of India would be Christian today."[7]

Today less than 3 percent of India's population is Christian. Hinduism is the largest religion in India and accounts for about 80 percent of the population. Islam is the second largest with about 13 percent.[8]

Rejection should never come because your life is not lining up with Christ's teachings. Know that when your deeds, your words, and your character consistently reflect the heart of Jesus and the gospel, it has the potential to have a far-reaching impact beyond anything you can imagine! Your faithful witness could transform an entire family, village, or country. So may we never "play the part," but be true and sincere followers of Christ.

Watch Closely

Imagine being a young Timothy and receiving a long-awaited letter from your mentor, the apostle Paul, with these words: "Watch your life and doctrine closely. Persevere in them, because if you do, you will save both yourself and your hearers" (1 Timothy 4:16).

Of course, Paul wrote much more to Timothy than this short passage, but it is a powerful verse to consider. Your life (*what you do*) and your doctrine (*what you believe*) have to line up. They must go hand in hand, Paul said, not only for your salvation, but also for the salvation of those who are listening to you.

There is perhaps no clearer definition for how Christ followers ought to conduct their lives than in Ephesians 4:22–32. In this passage, Paul wrote, "To put off your old self, which is being corrupted by its deceitful desires; to be made new in the attitude of your minds; and to put on the new self, created to be like God in true righteousness and holiness" (vv. 22–24).

He instructed believers to stop lying and to start speaking truthfully to one another; to put away anger; not to give the devil a foothold; not to steal but to work hard so that we have something to share with others. Lastly, he admonished in verses 29 through 32:

> Do not let any unwholesome talk come out of your mouths, but only what is helpful for building others up according to their needs, that it may benefit those who listen. And do not grieve the Holy Spirit of God, with whom you were sealed for the day of redemption. Get rid of all bitterness, rage and anger, brawling and slander, along with every form of malice. Be kind and compassionate to one another, forgiving each other, just as in Christ God forgave you.

When you read these words, do any personal habits or behaviors come to mind that you need to get rid of? I want to encourage you to spend a few minutes right now in prayer and ask the Lord if there's anything in your life that is not pleasing to Him, that might be hindering your witness to others. A good exercise is to have a pen and piece of paper ready so you can write down whatever comes to mind after you pray in the study question section below.

God may be telling you to put away anger, lust, greed, pride, or idleness. Whatever He might point out to you, please receive it with a humble heart. Then pray, and ask the Lord to give you the strength to eliminate these things for good, knowing that when God purifies our hearts and minds of all unrighteousness (1 John 1:9), others are able to see Christ in us more clearly.

Paul words and actions lined up with his doctrine. He lived and served humbly and did not hesitate to speak the truth. That's the same way you and I, through our words and actions, will paint a picture of Christ. Whether or not someone rejects that picture is out of our control; we just need to keep lifting up the name of Jesus in hopes that all people will be drawn to Him (John 12:32).

The Secret to Handling *No*

In many ways, learning how to handle a *no* is more important than learning how to handle a *yes*. The pain of rejection can derail many believers from their mission of preaching the gospel. Even worse, a mishandled *no* can ruin a relationship. Remember, just because a person says no to the gospel once doesn't mean they will always say no. Not everyone is like the fisherman I shared about earlier who refused my invitation again and again, so we must handle each *no* with patience and grace. And we mustn't give up.

Have you ever heard of the Red Lantern Award? It's a surprising medal given to one very specific participant in the famed Iditarod, a lengthy dogsledding race that spans over a thousand miles across Alaska. Every year the Red Lantern Award is given to the person who finishes last in the race. The person who finishes last gets an award! The Red Lantern actually started as a joke back in 1953 to poke fun at the person bringing up the rear, but now it has become a symbol of resilience and resolve. For a race that typically takes one to two weeks to finish, you need a lot of guts, and the Iditarod rewards that.[9]

Likewise, we also need resolve and resilience when it comes to telling others about Jesus. We absolutely cannot give up—no matter the obstacles we encounter and no matter how long it takes. There's too much at stake. We cannot let one *no* stand in the way of one hopeful and eventual *yes*. Therefore, we must learn how to handle the pain of rejection well, because if we can prove excellent in that regard, then we will be able to effectively pursue those who may be reluctant to accept the truth.

So how do we face rejection well, standing firm in our hope for and pursuit of lost souls?

We find this answer throughout the Word of God, but perhaps no place clearer than in the book of 1 Peter. Now, we should keep in mind that the apostle Peter wrote this letter to believers in the first century AD who were experiencing extreme persecution. There is a difference between being rejected because of Jesus and being persecuted because of Jesus, as we shall see in the next chapter. However, these believers were also experiencing rejection. Take a look at how Peter encouraged them:

> As you come to him, the living Stone—rejected by humans but chosen by God and precious to him—you also, like living stones, are being built into a spiritual house to be a holy priesthood, offering spiritual sacrifices acceptable to God through Jesus Christ. (1 Peter 2:4–5)

Remember earlier when we saw that Jesus was the rejected

cornerstone? Well, Peter went a step further and said that every single believer is a "living stone," like Jesus. As Jesus was rejected, so also His followers would be rejected, and they would need to understand how to deal with that rejection. As the apostle wrapped up his letter to Christians in 1 Peter 5:6–11, he gave us the steps for handling persecution, but they are also excellent steps for handling rejection:

1. Don't Take It Personal

In 1 Peter 5:6, the Bible says that believers were supposed to "humble yourselves, therefore, under God's mighty hand, that he may lift you up in due time." You might think that's a rather rude way to start this whole proceeding, but it's a necessary one. You cannot take yourself so seriously. Remember, when a person rejects your message, they're not rejecting you. They are rejecting the One who sent you.

Think about it this way: Have you ever met a good used-car salesman? Trust me, they're out there, and they all have one thing in common: they don't take themselves seriously. A used-car salesman cannot take it personally every time a customer refuses to buy a car. When salesmen think this way, they're difficult to talk to. They're always pressuring you, trying to get you to make a bad decision, trying to force you to take the stinker that has been sitting in the back corner of the lot for months and months.

But a good car salesman understands something very important: when a customer refuses to buy a car, it's the not the salesman they're rejecting; it's the car.

Listen, the gospel that you offer is the equivalent of offering the most expensive, most luxurious, most efficient vehicle in the world . . . for absolutely free. You are offering grace. You are offering Jesus, the Way to eternal life. If a person refuses that offer, it's likely not because your sales pitch isn't up to snuff. It's because they can't see the surprising, life-changing offer that is right in front of them. They're not rejecting you. They're rejecting Jesus.

2. Let God Handle Your Worries

Repeat after me: *Hakuna matata.* (It means "no worries.") You might think I'm kidding around or that I've watched *The Lion King* one too many times with my children, but that is basically what the Bible says! Look at the next verse, 1 Peter 5:7: "Cast all your anxiety on him because he cares for you." When Peter tells us to cast all our anxieties on the Lord, he means that we should take all of what bothers us in this world and what worries us and what gives us ulcers, and we should toss them away into the mighty and waiting hand of the Father.

> You are offering Jesus, the Way to eternal life. If a person refuses that offer.... It's because they can't see the surprising, life-changing offer that is right in front of them.

This includes every fear, worry, anxiety, or misgiving we may have about presenting the gospel and receiving rejection. Are you nervous that a person might say no? Don't worry about it. Cast your anxiety on the Lord. Are you anxious that a relationship might be ruined because you opened your mouth and told someone about Jesus? *Hakuna matata.* Give your distress to God.

Because, trust me, He can handle it. He created the world in seven days (technically six; he took a breather on the last one). He split the Red Sea in two. He raised His Son from the dead. I think He can handle a stomach full of butterflies.

Stop wasting time and energy fretting about how it's going to turn out. Give every twinge and ounce of nerves to God and do what you were called to do!

3. Keep a Clear Head and a Watchful Eye

This one is essential. Peter gave those believers a very stern and necessary warning in 1 Peter 5:8, one that we need to heed: "Be alert and of sober mind. Your enemy the devil prowls around like a roaring lion looking for someone to devour."

Rejection is a perfect opportunity for the enemy to strike. From Satan's point of view, it is an excellent moment to slither alongside you and whisper lies into your ear. He'll tell you all kinds of things: "You're not good enough. God is disappointed in you. Your friend will never speak to you again. You should leave evangelism to the pros."

All of those statements are lies meant to make you slip into the waiting jaws of the enemy. They will rip through your mind like tornados, trying to wreak as much havoc as possible.

So always be aware. With every failure and rejection, remind yourself that those statements are slivers of falsehood sent from the devil to infect you with doubt. Keep a cool head. Be logical. Don't let the devil, the "father of lies" (John 8:44), talk you out of sharing your faith.

4. Counter Falsehood with the Truth

Next, 1 Peter 5:9 tell us to resist the devil, "standing firm in the faith, because you know that the family of believers throughout the world is undergoing the same kind of sufferings." Yes, the devil is an expert liar and "the prince of this world" (John 12:31). But the Bible also says in 1 John 4:4, "The one who is in you is greater than the one who is in the world." Who is in us? The Holy Spirit! And He is greater than the evil one. Moreover, the Holy Spirit gives us the power to resist the devil and to stand firm in the faith despite rejection and persecution.

Every time you are presented with a lie causing you to fear rejection, remember that you have within you the Holy Spirit who, as Jesus promised, "will teach you all things and will remind you of everything I have said to you" (John 14:26). Remember what is true, from God's Word, and it will help you battle rejection.

5. After Time, God Will Restore You

The final step is a promise we can hold on to: "And the God of all grace, who called you to his eternal glory in Christ, after you have suffered a little while, will himself restore you and make you strong, firm and steadfast" (1 Peter 5:10). And what a marvelous promise, one that gives us hope! To *restore* means to "set into order." Just like God formed the universe and set everything into order (Hebrews 11:3), He will also set everything right in your life. The rejection you experience will be met with His acceptance. Your failure will be met with His triumph.

So relax. God has you in His hands. He will protect you and keep you safe.

I know rejection hurts. I've felt its sting more than once. I still think about my fisherman friend from the opening of this chapter who refused to come to church to hear the good news. I still remember that news story on the television set, telling me I had run out of chances.

But God will restore your hope. He will strengthen you for the task He has set before you, even if you get rejected on the first, third, or seventh try. Sometimes that rejection can be downright persecution. We're going to explore that difficult topic next because it is an essential step in your journey.

DISCUSSION QUESTIONS

1. Read Ephesians 4:22–32. When you read these words, what personal habits or behaviors come to mind that you need to get rid of? How does following through with this exercise help you to "watch your life and doctrine closely" as instructed in 1 Timothy 4:16? According to the apostle Paul, what will be the end result if you do?

2. Think back on a time when you felt the pain of rejection. How did you handle this situation?

3. Read Matthew 10:11–15. What does Jesus tell His disciples to do when they face rejection? How does this encourage you to share your faith regardless of your circumstances?

4. Read Luke 10:16. According to this verse, when someone rejects the gospel, who are they actually rejecting? How does this help you not to take rejection personally?

5. How can your closeness with God help you to get past the rejection you experience?

6. How does walking with someone through his or her acceptance of Christ help you forget the sting of rejection you have felt in the past or will feel in the future?

CHAPTER 13

Count the Cost

"When Christ was in the world, He was despised by men. . . .
He had enemies and defamers; do you want everyone
to be your friend, your benefactor? How can your patience
be rewarded if no adversity test it? How can you be
a friend of Christ if you are not willing to suffer any hardship?
Suffer with Christ and for Christ if you wish to reign with Him."

THOMAS À KEMPIS

Preaching the gospel isn't always a safe endeavor. At times, your reputation, your well-being, and even your life could be at stake. According to 2 Timothy 3:12, "In fact, everyone who wants to live a godly life in Christ Jesus will be persecuted."

The Bible says that this is a fact. It's not a "might happen" kind of scenario. There isn't a chance that you'll squeak by unscathed. Jesus tells us in no uncertain terms in Matthew 24:9 that you "will be handed over to be persecuted and put to death, and [you] will be hated by all nations because of me." Since we represent Jesus as His ambassadors, we will be treated as Jesus was treated.

Paul wrote in Ephesians 6:12, "For our struggle is not against flesh and blood, but against the rulers, against the authorities, against the powers of this dark world and against the spiritual forces of evil in the heavenly realms." This means, as we touched on in chapters 2 and 6, that while it may appear that a person is against you because of the gospel, there is a behind-the-scenes battle going on. The root, the source, the underlying opposition is actually spiritual.

In John 15:18, Jesus told His disciples, "If the world hates you, keep in mind that it hated me first." And He said later,

> If they persecuted me, they will persecute you also. If they obeyed my teaching, they will obey yours also. They will treat you this way because of my name, for they do not know the one who sent me. (vv. 20–21)

Why does this happen?

It happens because the message of the cross offends people. The Son of God confronts humanity with their sin. His truth shines a floodlight on darkness, and that makes people uncomfortable—even hostile or angry. So, instead of reaching out for salvation, people may mistreat you. They may ridicule, or hurt you to get you to stop sharing the good news. Let's look at some modern-day examples.

"I Am a Christian"

Persecution happens all over the world. We see it in Somalia, in Iraq and Syria, in Afghanistan and Pakistan, in North Korea and China. We know for a fact there are over sixty countries around the world where Christians are being persecuted as I write. We know that every year, tens of thousands of believers die for their faith.

A man named Habila Adamu knows what it means to

experience persecution. The Boko Haram entered his house with AK-47s, asked his name and his profession, and then they asked if he was a Christian.

"I am a Christian," he replied.

They told him that he needed to forsake his faith and to repeat these words: "There is no god but Allah, and Muhammad is his messenger." They told him that they were giving him an opportunity to live and to lead a blessed life.

He refused. "I am a Christian and will always remain a Christian," he replied, "even to death."

One of the men put the barrel of his AK-47 in Habila's mouth and pulled the trigger. Habila fell. After that house the Boko Haram proceeded to enter thirty other homes of those who attended Habila's church. They systematically killed every person in each house.

But then, somehow, while lying in a pool of his own blood, Habila began to move. Somehow that bullet did not kill him, although it did leave him on the edge of life. Praise the Lord, Habila ended up surviving the attack.[1]

A fellow pastor and friend of mine named Ajai Lall told me a story regarding the persecution that is taking place in India. He shared about a man named Sanjay who wished to be a pastor. Sanjay traveled to central India to a place controlled by extremists. There were no Christian churches whatsoever in that area, so Sanjay went there and began to preach. At the end of one year, he had some three hundred people attending his church.

But on March 25, 2007, he was surrounded and attacked and beaten severely by extremists. He was sent to the hospital, unconscious and in critical condition. Several days later, he woke up in the ICU. He asked for his wife, Goshan, but only received terrible news in return. While he was unconscious, the extremists who had beaten him also beat his wife. She did not survive. Her funeral had already taken place.

About a month later, Sanjay returned to the area where he resumed preaching the gospel. He went back to that same area of India that had claimed his wife.

Faith on Trial

The persecution Habila and Sanjay suffered is taking place all over the world. Not only is it happening all over the world, it's beginning to happen in the United States of America! That might surprise you, but it's true.

I read recently about a nineteen-year veteran in the United States Air Force who was placed under a new commanding officer who happened to be a lesbian. His commanding officer asked him about his views on same-sex marriage. The veteran replied that he did not believe his opinion on the matter got in the way of doing his job. She insisted that he answer the question. As a Christian, he said, he believed that a marriage was only between a man and a woman. Because of his answer, he was immediately relieved of his duties.[2]

A federal judge threatened to incarcerate a high school valedictorian unless she removed all references to Jesus in her speech.[3] In another city, officials prohibited senior citizens from praying over their meals at the senior citizen center.[4]

In Portland, Maine, three Muslim men murdered a forty-nine-year-old Christian man. He was found beaten to death, with blood splattered on the Bible that was on his bedside table. This did not happen in the Middle East. It happened in the United States.[5]

Friend, persecution in the world is a present reality. At this moment there are people who stand against your message, and some will do whatever it takes to stop you.

But don't be alarmed. This has been happening for a long time, and it will continue to happen until the Lord returns. It hasn't stopped the church yet. In fact, the opposite is true.

Nevertheless

I want to take you on a quick journey through the book of Acts. By the end I believe we'll see something very surprising. The church begins in Acts 2:41. Peter had just finished preaching the very first evangelistic sermon ever. He told those who had gathered in Jerusalem for Pentecost about Jesus Christ and the forgiveness of sins that He offers. The Bible says, "Those who accepted his message were baptized, and about three thousand were added to their number that day."

Three thousand people is not a bad start for the first day! Verse 47 says that the church was "praising God and enjoying the favor of all the people. And the Lord added to their number daily those who were be-ing saved." Notice that the church didn't just grow on Sundays; it grew every day of the week. Their number was growing daily.

> Persecution in the world is a present reality. At this moment there are people who stand against your message, and some will do whatever it takes to stop you.

In Acts chapter 3, we read about a paralyzed man who was begging at the gate called Beautiful and was healed by Peter and John. Those two disciples, through the power of the Holy Spirit, enabled him to walk. You would think that the authorities would have been happy about this. You would think that they would have been overjoyed. But you'd be wrong.

Sadly, the authorities didn't want anything to do with Jesus. And they began to persecute those who had healed this man. Acts 4:1–2 tells us:

The priests and the captain of the temple guard and the Sadducees came up to Peter and John while they were speaking to the people. They were greatly disturbed because the apostles were teaching the people, proclaiming in Jesus the resurrection of the dead.

The authorities seized the apostles and put them in jail. So now we have Christians being jailed for healing a paralyzed man and for telling the truth of the gospel. Despite the good that the apostles were doing, they were still mistreated. They were persecuted for their faith and for their preaching. But here's the surprising thing: persecution didn't slow the church. Look at what Acts 4:4 says:

But many who heard the message believed; so the number of men who believed grew to about five thousand.

Despite the efforts of the authorities in Jerusalem to silence the gospel, the church continued to grow. This growth worried a particular group of authorities in Jerusalem called the Sanhedrin. From history we know that the Sanhedrin was a council of key religious and political leaders who gathered to settle major cases or argue interpretations of the Law.[6] In fact, we learn in Matthew 26:57–68 that the Sanhedrin was the group of men responsible for handing over Jesus to the Romans to be crucified.

So in Acts 4:17, because Peter and John were preaching the gospel, the Sanhedrin said to each other, ". . . to stop this thing from spreading any further among the people, we must warn them to speak no longer to anyone in this name [of Jesus Christ]." Then, in the very next verse, they commanded Peter and John to stop speaking and teaching in the name of Jesus and threatened them.

Now, was that the moment when the church disbanded and everyone went home? Was that the point when the apostles hung it up and decided that the gospel wasn't worth preaching?

Nope. That's not what happened at all.

Acts 5:14 says, "Nevertheless"—oh, how I love that word!—"more and more men and women believed in the Lord and were added to their number."

Unstoppable Force

Just a few verses later, in Acts 5:18, we see that the apostles were arrested and placed in the public jail. It was no longer just threats. The Sanhedrin were going to do something about their message. Maybe imprisonment was enough to deter the apostles? But verses 19 and 20 say:

> During the night an angel of the Lord opened the doors of the jail and brought them out. "Go, stand in the temple courts," he said, "and tell the people all about this new life."

The apostles did as the angel told them. They went right back to the temple courts the very next morning to preach again about Jesus. You can't stop the church!

But look what happens in Acts 5:40: "[The Sanhedrin] called the apostles in and had them flogged. Then they ordered them not to speak in the name of Jesus, and let them go."

This was getting serious now. It wasn't just prison. The physical well-being of the apostles was at stake.

So what was the church's reaction to all of this? Verse 41 says that the apostles left the Sanhedrin "rejoicing because they had been counted worthy of suffering disgrace for the Name." They didn't stop teaching or proclaiming the name of Jesus (v. 42). Indeed, the very opposite was true. They continued to meet day after day, and not just in the temple courts; they went from house to house. Every day they met. Every day they taught from the Word of God. Every day they proclaimed the truth that Jesus was Lord and that He had risen from the dead.

Undeniable Cause and Effect

Then something happened in Acts chapter 6. A man named Stephen came onto the scene. He was a deacon selected by the apostles to ensure that food was being distributed equally among the widows in Jerusalem (vv. 1–6). Stephen used that authority as a platform by which to work miraculous signs among the people and to preach the gospel (v. 8). But his preaching and work among the people infuriated the religious leaders of Jerusalem so much that they brought him before the Sanhedrin to be tried (v. 9–15).

In Acts 7, Stephen gave a passionate plea to the Sanhedrin. He unfolded before them the history of Israel, beginning all the way from Father Abraham to Moses and the Exodus to King Solomon and the prophets. He challenged the Sanhedrin to receive the message to which all of the history of Israel pointed—the truth that Jesus is the Messiah and that He came to save the world. But the Sanhedrin refused.

All together, they rushed Stephen, dragged him outside of the city, and stoned him to death.

He was the first martyr of the church, the first man who died because of the message of the gospel. He was the first of millions who would die for their faith. From Stephen's death, the Bible says in Acts 8:1 that "a great persecution broke out against the church at Jerusalem, and all except the apostles were scattered throughout Judea and Samaria."

Now, at this point in our journey I want to take a moment and point out something interesting in that verse.

To where exactly did everyone (except the apostles) scatter? To Judea and Samaria. Keep those two places in mind. This might seem like a strange thing to do, but I want you to switch the numbers in that chapter and verse. I promise this isn't a magic trick. This is something much more profound than that.

Take a look at what it says in Acts 1:8. In that verse, the very beginning of the story of the church, Jesus told His disciples before He ascended into heaven, "You will receive power when the Holy Spirit comes on you; and you will be my witnesses in Jerusalem, and in all Judea and Samaria, and to the ends of the earth."

Whoa, there are those two places again—Judea and Samaria. Let me ask you a question: Prior to this great persecution that occurred in Acts 8:1, had the gospel been preached in Judea and Samaria? According to what we have read, not at all. In chapter 2, when the apostle Peter preached the gospel for the very first time, that sermon took place in Jerusalem. In chapter 3, when Peter preached again, it was in Jerusalem. In chapters 4, 5, 6, and 7, the gospel had only been preached in Jerusalem.

But now, because of this great persecution in Acts 8:1, believers had been spread to where? *To Judea and Samaria.* Acts 8:4 tells us: "Those who had been scattered preached the word wherever they went."

Do you realize what just happened? Until that great persecution, the gospel had not begun to spread. However, because the church was persecuted, it spread. And because the church spread, the gospel spread along with it. First to Judea. Then to Samaria. And finally to the ends of the earth.

Do you realize the same is true today? The persecution of

the church remains one of the most powerful means by which the gospel spreads. A theologian from the second century AD, a man named Tertullian, put it brilliantly when he famously wrote, "The blood of the martyrs is the seed of the church."

Unquenchable Fire

One of the most inspiring stories I have ever heard is one of a North Korean woman by the name of Kim Eun Jin. Growing up as the daughter of secret believers in Pyongyang, North Korea, she knew that if anyone discovered her and her family's Christian faith, they would likely be punished by the political regime. She was often asked by her family to stand outside of their apartment to keep watch while a group of believers prayed inside. Her father repeatedly told her they would pay a price for their faith.

> The persecution of the church remains one of the most powerful means by which the gospel spreads.

Nevertheless, her father said, "Even if I face death I will follow Jesus."

In 1994, the police discovered that her father was leading an underground church and promptly arrested him during a raid. That was the last time Kim Eun Jin saw her father. She never learned what happened to him. Her best guess is that he was sent to one of the six labor camps in North Korea and possibly executed.

Kim's mother, grandmother, and siblings escaped to the mountains. In 2005, a Chinese pastor helped Kim cross the Tumen River. She defected to China, and her family followed a short time later.[7]

Despite her father's death, Kim Eun Jin has a dream. She wants to return to North Korea. She wants to go back to the place where her father died and preach the very same gospel that claimed his life.

She wants to share the love of God with the people of North Korea.

"We are getting ready for that day when the doors open," she said.[8]

What a remarkable testimony. You'd think that the fear of death would deter a woman like Kim Eun Jin. You'd think that the death of her father would keep her from preaching the gospel. But the opposite is true. She cannot wait to return. There is a fire in her that cannot be quenched.

Three Truths to Remember

Persecution is always difficult. It challenges what we as believers can handle and what we are willing to endure. It can rattle the very foundation of our faith.

There are no how-to steps for dealing with persecution. There's no plan or program for making it through unscathed. But there are truths we can remember—promises that God has made that serve as candles of hope pointing us forward through dark times in our lives. In particular, I believe there are three truths that can give us courage to face our opposition:

1. Jesus Knows Exactly What You're Going Through

There is no wound on this earth that our Lord does not understand, for He bore them all on the cross. He knows the physical and emotional toll that His believers sustain. When you read in Scripture the medical aspects of Jesus's crucifixion, you notice that He suffered these five very distinct wounds:

- **A contused wound.** A blow from a blunt instrument. Micah 5:1 tells us that Jesus was hit with a rod on His cheek.

- **A lacerated wound.** A tearing abrasion, such as the wound inflicted by the whip topped with metal and ivory that tore into Jesus's back. Such suffering was unfathomable. Isaiah 50:6 records that Jesus "offered [His] back to those who beat [Him]."
- **A penetrating wound.** Prior to Jesus's crucifixion, Roman soldiers mocked His claim as "King of the Jews" by placing a crown of four-inch thorns upon His head (Matthew 27:29). Securing this crown to Jesus's head would have resulted in a deep, circulate of wounds.
- **A perforating wound.** Jesus endured the excruciating pain of iron nails being pierced through His body, driven between His bones to separate but not break them (Psalm 22:16).
- **An incision.** Much like a surgeon using a scalpel, incisions are caused by sharp-edged instruments. While Jesus hung on the cross whipped, beaten, and bruised, a soldier pierced His side, producing a flow of blood and water (John 19:34).

Jesus knew the pain of human suffering on the cross. He experienced the result of bringing grace and truth to the world. Whatever pain we may face for sharing the gospel, whether physical or emotional or spiritual, we should keep in mind that Jesus understands it full well. We worship a God who understands what we're going through and who sees what we face on account of Him.

2. God Is Able to Use a Bad Situation for Your Good
Many believers know the story of Joseph in the book of Genesis. Out of jealousy, his brothers faked his death and sold him into

slavery. The wife of his slave master accused him of trying to seduce her, a charge that was untrue, and got him thrown into prison. While in prison, he interpreted the dreams of a baker and a cup-bearer, and later, Pharaoh, and as a result, became the second-in-command of all of Egypt. When his brothers came to Egypt begging for food, they did not recognize Joseph even as they stood in his presence. Instead of sending them to their deaths out of revenge, he had pity on them and forgave them.

After their father, Jacob, died, Joseph's brothers became nervous. They were terrified by the notion that the only reason Joseph was choosing to be nice to them was out of love for his father. But now that his father had died, they feared he would finally exact his revenge. But Joseph reassured their fears and delivered a powerful biblical truth.

He said to them in Genesis 50:20, "You intended to harm me, but God intended it for good to accomplish what is now being done, the saving of many lives." This scripture should be the Martyr's Anthem.

Listen, some people will hate you because of your message. Some people will make fun of you. Some people may even choose to hurt you. Their intentions are evil. But God's intentions are good, and He has the power to transform the evil that the world does into the good of those who love Him (Romans 8:28).

3. Persecution Is One of the Greatest Opportunities for Evangelism

In his seminal book *The Rise of Christianity*, a secular sociologist named Rodney Stark pointed out that the greatest possible testimony for faith came from those who were willing to give up their lives. One of the reasons why Christianity spread so quickly through the Roman Empire was because very few could doubt that

Christians were serious about what they believed since they were willing to give up their lives.

In an earlier chapter, I shared with you 1 Peter 3:15 about sharing Christ with gentleness and respect, but now let's look at the full paragraph as it relates to persecution:

> Who is going to harm you if you are eager to do good? But even if you should suffer for what is right, you are blessed. . . . In your hearts revere Christ as Lord. Always be prepared to give an answer to everyone who asks you to give the reason for the hope that you have. But do this with gentleness and respect, keeping a clear conscience, so that those who speak maliciously against your good behavior in Christ may be ashamed of their slander. (vv. 13–16)

Even if you suffer for doing right, you are blessed! When you are gentle and respectful in sharing the truth, the Bible says that eventually the person who slanders you will be ashamed of what they've said about you.

A Miraculous Conversion

Remember that journey we took through Acts earlier? I left out one very important part to the story. There was a man who oversaw the death of Stephen, the first Christian martyr. His name was Saul (Acts 8:1), a Pharisee from Tarsus. The Bible says he was one of the fiercest persecutors of Christians in Judea and in Samaria. He dragged men and women believers from their homes and threw them into prison. He was responsible for their deaths.

Saul was on a road to Damascus, on his way to persecute the Christians who were living there, when a bright light stopped him in his tracks. There was a man standing in the midst of that bright light who had a question for Saul.

He asked, "Saul, Saul, why do you persecute me?" (Acts 9:4).

When Saul asked who was speaking to him, the voice replied, "I am Jesus, whom you are persecuting. Now get up and go into the city, and you will be told what you must do" (vv. 5–6).

That moment was a turning point for Saul, who later became the apostle for the Lord Jesus known as Paul, the man responsible for writing one third of the books of the New Testament. It was at that moment that Saul realized what he was doing, that he was standing against God and against his beloved ones.

History is full of stories of those who persecuted Christians and then later believed their message. Saul's story happens time and time again. Why? Because of the courage and endurance that believers have shown through their trials. That kind of strength can't be found anywhere else in the world. It can only be found in Jesus.

So, if you ever face persecution, remember that your Lord understands your struggle. He is able to turn your suffering into good. And He will make a way for you to share the truth that lives inside your heart for the saving of many lives.

In 2 Corinthians 4:17–18, Paul wrote a beautiful reminder for us all when it comes to suffering for our faith. I shared part of this Scripture in chapter 4, the eternity chapter, but it bears repeating in full:

> For our light and momentary troubles are achieving for us
> an eternal glory that far outweighs them all. So we fix our

eyes not on what is seen, but on what is unseen, since what is seen is temporary, but what is unseen is eternal.

What this means is that, in comparison with the unfathomable span of eternity, our suffering on earth is "light and momentary." Isn't that an amazing perspective? And even better than that, Paul declared that our troubles are working together to achieve glory for *eternity* that far outweighs anything we may be enduring today.

It is important that we count the cost of following Jesus and sharing His message with the world. But what we learn from Scripture is that persecution and suffering are well worth the victory that will someday be ours—when, after faithfully enduring and crossing that finish line, we enter into our reward. This reward is an eternity spent with our loving Father and the people who led us to Him . . . and all the people who led them to Him . . . and all the people we led to Him . . . and so on, and so on.

DISCUSSION QUESTIONS

1. What are some things that frighten you about persecution?

2. Trust is a process. The more you trust God with your fears, the more you will see that He will be with you every step of your journey, never leaving nor forsaking you. What area of life do you fear giving over to God? Why do you fear this process with God?

3. How will handing your fears over to God help you to better suffer for your faith?

4. Read Luke 9:23. How does this verse further reveal the seriousness of following Jesus? How does this verse tie into the theme of this chapter?

5. Read 1 Peter 4:16. How do you perceive other people who are able to suffer for their faith? What kind of attraction do you have toward them? How do you think others perceive you with your ability to suffer for your faith?

6. During your prayer time with God, ask Him to strengthen and encourage you to be able to withstand the difficulties of sharing your faith. Ask Him to give you the desire to share your faith and suffer with the same heart that Jesus had.

CHAPTER 14

Time
to Celebrate

"You are not fighting for victory—
you are fighting from victory.
This battle has already been won!"

TONY EVANS

There is no victory on this earth that compares to leading a person to Jesus. I promise you, from the very bottom of my heart, there is nothing like it. Winning a race, even one as difficult and renowned as the Tour de France, does not compare to it. Knocking out an opponent in a boxing ring, or catching a pass for a touchdown, or scoring the winning basket as the shot clock strikes zero—none of those victories compare to it. Nor does making a billion dollars or winning the presidency of the United States or blasting off into outer space.

There is no victory anywhere in this universe that comes close to the victory we witness when a person decides to follow Christ. Every time—every single time—it brings me tears of joy.

A Park Bench in Hermosa Beach

The bicycle route along Hermosa Beach is one of my favorite rides because of its peaceful, scenic beauty. In Spanish, the word *hermosa* literally means "beautiful." Truly, it's like something out of a movie. Even on the hottest days, there's always a breeze coming in from the ocean, and more importantly, there are plenty of places to stop and rest.

You can also meet some pretty interesting people in Hermosa Beach. In fact, the closer you get to the Pacific Ocean, the more interesting people typically get. You'll see characters of all kinds: hippies trapped in the seventies, intimidating bodybuilders, costumed heroes riding on skateboards. If you stopped one person on the way to chat for a bit, you'd never be able to guess at the story you'd hear.

While I was riding in Hermosa Beach one afternoon, I decided to take a rest at one stop adjacent to the path. There was a park bench there, and sitting on the bench was an elderly woman—a woman I would soon come to know as Peggy.

"Do you mind if I sit here?" I asked her.

"No, I don't mind," she replied with a raspy, East Coast accent.

I sat down next to her and took in the view of the horizon as my body began to cool down from the ride. It didn't take me long to strike up a conversation with the woman. Small talk at first, but then I asked, "How old are you?"

"I'm ninety-nine years old," she replied. There was a note of feisty confidence in her tone.

"Ninety-nine?" I exclaimed. "How are you ninety-nine?"

"I'm petrified," she said.

"Petrified?" I asked. "What do you mean you're petrified?"

She told me, "Well, I used to own a bar down in Long Beach, and I drank for twenty years. So now all my body parts are petrified."

She caught my full attention with that line. Even from this brief conversation with her, I knew that this was no ordinary lady.

"Well, how old do you think I am?" I inquired.

"Oh, you're like, I don't know, maybe thirty-eight?" She said some real low number like that. Now, she may not have been able to tell from looking at me that I was actually much older than my late thirties because I was wearing sunglasses and a bicycle helmet.

But I said, "I love you so much."

We laughed and continued to talk for a while. She was swearing and telling jokes. Eventually she asked me what I did for a living, and I told her that I was a preacher. She about fell over right there from a heart attack. She could not believe I was a preacher.

Peggy's Birthday

I learned a lot about Peggy after that meeting on a bench near the road in Hermosa Beach. Besides owning a bar and drinking for many years, I learned that though she had a Catholic background, her life had deviated far from her faith. It had been a long time since she had even thought about God.

After that day at the beach, I kept in touch with Peggy. We quickly became friends. Through our friendship, she became interested in Jesus Christ and in the church. Although she wanted to come to Shepherd Church, she couldn't drive at her age, so she started watching our services on TV.

Shortly thereafter—at the age of ninety-nine—Peggy accepted Jesus as her Lord and Savior. She had a true, major conversion experience in her life. Everything in her life changed as she made a decision to spend the remaining years of her life following Christ. She would spend all day every day writing letters to the other elderly people in her retirement community, encouraging them. Her letters were filled with Bible verses.

I had the privilege of surprising Peggy at her hundredth birthday party. She had no idea I was coming. As I walked into a large dining room at her retirement home, I saw more than a hundred people there. At one table were all her doctors. A boatload of doctors. Another table was filled with her friends from the retirement home. Her family was there as well.

When I arrived, Peggy was up at the front of the room speaking, talking about her life and what had become most important to her. Since everyone there was a stranger to me, I decided to stay toward the back of the room, listen to Peggy, and watch the party unfold. I wasn't there long before this little lady came up to me. She looked sort of awestruck, and then meekly she asked, "Are you Pastor Dudley?"

"Yes," I said. *How does she know who I am?* I wondered.

She told me that she had been watching my sermons on television, all because of Peggy. She said I ought to follow her to the stage to go say hello to Peggy.

"No, no, no," I said. "I shouldn't interrupt her."

"Oh, no, she would want me to interrupt her for you," the lady insisted.

So she led me though the room to Peggy. As I walked up to her, she looked up at me with the biggest smile. "Oh, my Dudley!" she said.

Peggy introduced me to the crowd and asked me to tell them the story of how we met, so I did. It was a wonderful evening celebrating this beautiful soul. She was a firecracker, and everyone enjoyed reminiscing about the funny and loving ways she had touched their lives. You don't meet someone like Peggy every day.

While I was writing this book, Peggy passed away. She knew I was including her story in one of the chapters, but I wish I had been able to show it to her before she died. The important thing is the fondness we shared for one another and that Peggy was a passionate follower of Jesus who spent her remaining years telling people about Jesus with her trademark gusto.

She left this world at the age of 102. Her passing was not a loss. It was anything but, because she went on to glory. She entered into eternity with the Lord.

Peggy's life was a victory, and watching her make that change in her life—even at the age of ninety-nine—is one of the greatest honors of my life. When I think about her and how her whole life changed, I can't help but smile. Her story reminds me again and again why I am so compelled to share the gospel. The change in her life is proof that every ounce of blood, sweat, and tears believers in Christ put into this good work of evangelism is worth it.

It's never too late to lead a person to Jesus. And it's never too late for a person to accept Jesus into his or her heart.

A God-Honored Guarantee

Wouldn't it be great to have a written guarantee from God that your work in evangelism will result in victory—that people around you will become saved? Would it be an extra motivation to get busy telling people about Jesus?

> Peggy's life was a victory, and watching her make that change in her life–even at the age of ninety-nine– is one of the greatest honors of my life.

Well, guess what? There *is* a God-honored guarantee! Read what Psalm 126:6 says: "Those who goes out weeping, carrying seed to sow, will return with songs of joy, carrying sheaves with them."

How much more assurance do we need? The Bible says that God has promised a return on our spiritual investment. But there are requirements. Notice the four things we have to do for God's promise to work:

- We must go to a lost world.
- We must weep over lost people.
- We must carry the seed.
- We must sow.

All four are necessary—*go, weep, carry,* and *sow*—to receive that guarantee. Simply going to a lost world isn't enough. The tears that fall from our eyes aren't enough. Just carrying the seed of God's Word is not enough.

Listen, you could fly halfway around the world to a place that doesn't know Jesus. You could spend your days and nights weeping on behalf of a lost world. And you could know the Bible backward and forward in three different versions. Those are all good and honorable things. But it does us no good if we do not go out and sow the gospel. We will not be able to celebrate if we do not sow the seed.

Because remember what the Bible says: when you sow God's Word, it always accomplishes what it is sent out to do (Isaiah 55:11).

In Matthew 13, Jesus compared preaching the Word of God to a farmer who went out to sow seed in the fields. Sometimes your seed falls on hard ground (meaning the Word falls on a hard heart), and the birds come and take it away. Other times the ground is rocky. That person will have some interest in God but there is no root system to sustain it. Sometimes the ground is full of thorns. A person will hear the Word, but the temptations of the world will choke it away.

This will happen. But it's okay. We need to keep sowing the seed because we will eventually come across a heart that is open and receptive. Jesus referred to this type of person as "good soil," someone who is primed and ready to receive the Word. And when that person receives the Word and allows it to take root, the harvest and victory that we reap will surprise you. Jesus said in Matthew 13:8 that the crop we reap will be "a hundred, sixty or thirty times what was sown."

Can you imagine that? Much of your work might seem like a failure. Many people will reject the gospel. But victory is promised! God has given us a guarantee that we will reap thirty, sixty, and even one hundred times what we have sown! So keep sowing! God will absolutely and unequivocally bring about a harvest. You will bring a spiritual return, the lost souls who have been brought into the kingdom of God.

A Street Called George

Years ago, I read a story about an English preacher who was interrupted in the middle of his sermon by a man who wanted to give his testimony. The preacher permitted him to talk, and the man began to tell how he got saved. While in Sydney, Australia, on a street called George, a small, old, white-haired man had handed him a gospel tract and said, "Excuse me, sir, are you saved? If you died tonight, are you going to heaven?" After reading the pamphlet and wrestling with the elderly man's words, the young man had accepted Jesus into his heart.

That was quite a story. But here's the surprising thing: that preacher kept hearing that same story over and over again.

As the preacher traveled to different countries around the world, he would hear this same testimony over and over again, from random people who came to know Christ in Sydney, Australia, on a street called George, because a small, old man had handed them a tract. One day this preacher knew he had to meet the person who was affecting the lives of so many from around the world. So he traveled to Sydney, Australia, to a street called George.

Walking up and down the streets, he began to ask people, "Do you know of a little white-haired man who hands out Bible tracts here?"

Finally, a fellow Christian worker pointed him in the right direction. "Yes, his name is Frank Jenner," he said. "I'll take you to where he lives." When the preacher found the man's residence, he knocked, and the small white-haired man opened the door and invited him in. During their visit, the preacher asked, "Sir, why exactly do you hand out these tracts?"

Frank answered, "Forty years ago I lived a reprobate life, and someone cared enough about me to hand me a tract. It changed my life forever, and I made a promise to God that I would hand out at least ten tracts a day for the rest of my life."

Overwhelmed by his dedication, the visiting preacher began to explain just how effective his efforts had been. People from all over the world had been saved in Sydney, Australia, on a street called George. Then the frail, old man did something that caught the preacher completely off guard. He began to cry.

"Up until this moment," Frank said, "I never knew if it had ever done anyone any good. For forty years I've never been told that anybody ever came to Christ as a result of my tracts!"

The preacher told him, "Sir, by my calculations, the number of people you have influenced for Jesus Christ over the years would be more than 146,000!"[1]

To many, Frank Jenner looked like a peculiar white-haired man who spent every day of the latter part of his life approaching strangers with a compelling question and religious propaganda. He pressed on, despite discouragement and disappointment—and despite seeing zero results for his efforts for many years. "What a waste of time," some might surmise. "What a loser," others might declare. "Too bad it was all for nothing," still others might decide.

However, through Frank Jenner's faithfulness, a sum of people totaling the population of a small city were brought to Jesus. His were the tears of a man who had realized his work had accomplished something truly great for the kingdom of God. And in the scope of eternity—not in the scope of worldly, temporary definitions of success—Frank's story is not one of a man who wasted his life on the streets of George. Frank's story is one of victory.

But God

Sometimes victory is nowhere in sight. You may pray for and share the gospel with someone countless times, and it may look as though they will never, ever give their heart to Jesus. It may be tempting to throw in the towel. To give up hope.

But God.

No, that's not a typo.

Repeat after me, "But God."

Oftentimes in the Bible we see these two short words preceding a great victory. This little phrase, "but God," occurs sixty times in the New International Version of the Bible. I love what the late pastor and author Ray C. Stedman once wrote about this:

> If you want a wonderful experience, take your New Testament and use a concordance to look up the two little words, "but God." See how many times human resources have been brought to an utter end; despair has gripped the heart and pessimism and gloom has settled upon a people; and there is nothing that can be done. Then see how the Spirit of God writes in luminous letters, but God, and the whole situation changes into victory.[2]

One of my favorite instances of this phrase is in Psalm 74:8–13.

The psalmist spoke of a terrible time in Israel's history where their enemies were seemingly victorious over them. He wrote that these enemies of God burned His sanctuary to the ground—in fact, "every place where God was worshiped in the land" was burned, according to verse 8. Sadly, God's people were given no signs from Him, and there were no prophets left. No one knew how long this trial would last, how long their foes would mock and revile God.

> *But God* is my King from long ago;
>   he brings salvation on the earth. (Psalm 74:12)

The psalmist then told of God's awesome power to save. However powerful their foes may have seemed, the psalmist acknowledged that *God* was the One who split the sea and crushed the head of Leviathan (a monstrous sea creature) and opened up streams and rivers. The day and night belong to Him. He "set all the boundaries of the earth" (v. 17). The psalmist asked God to remember His covenant and appealed to His great mercy, and we know from reading the Old Testament that the Lord was merciful to His people and showed up mightily on their behalf time and time again.

Another one of my favorite places that "but God" appears in the Bible is in Acts 2:22–24. At the day of Pentecost, the Holy Spirit came upon a group of believers who were gathered in Jerusalem. As a result, they began speaking in tongues, and some of the God-fearing Jews among them thought they were drunk. Then Peter stood up with the other eleven disciples and addressed the crowd. He said,

> Fellow Israelites, listen to this: Jesus of Nazareth was a
> man accredited by God to you by miracles, wonders and

signs, which God did among you through him, as you yourselves know. This man was handed over to you by God's deliberate plan and foreknowledge; and you, with the help of wicked men, put him to death by nailing him to the cross. *But God* raised him from the dead, freeing him from the agony of death, because it was impossible for death to keep its hold on him.

Light came into the world (John 3:19), and people tried to stomp out that Light. It almost looked as though they were successful, but God had a different plan. But God stepped in. But God raised Jesus from the dead, and through that extraordinary miracle, He made a way for everyone who believes in His Son to also be raised from the dead and have everlasting life.

That same power brings salvation to the world. Even in the most hopeless situations, the Lord God Almighty can make a way. As you share the gospel and you aren't sure whether or not people will ever be saved, remember the two words that change everything in an instance: *but God.*

Not by Accident

There's one last word I want to share with you, but before I do that, I need to tell you one last story. It's about a man named Phil.

The first time I met Phil was on a Tuesday night in September after he crashed his bicycle right in front of me. Have you ever seen a bicycle crash on television during the Olympics or the Tour de France? In an instant, everything changes for that one cyclist or the multiple cyclists involved. One moment they are speeding down the road at twenty-five miles per hour; the next moment, they suddenly collide into the asphalt as onlookers wait with gripped hearts and bated breath to learn the prognosis.

While there are real dangers to road cycling, I took up the sport a few years ago after a knee injury. Cycling is a fun and challenging exercise that's low impact on one's knees. I can ride for hours, enjoying God's magnificent creation. Any stress I might be carrying disappears as soon as the wind hits my face.

Every week I go out riding with a group of guys, usually on Saturday morning before our evening church service. One week I couldn't make it, so I joined a group that rides on Tuesday nights instead.

Many of these cyclists in the Tuesday-night group have been riding for almost forty years now. Typically, they do a big loop through the San Fernando Valley, starting at the California State University Northridge (CSUN) campus and then swinging around on Mulholland before coming up on De Soto.

About twenty to thirty guys went out that Tuesday night. The traffic was thick, and we were riding close to each other like a swarm of bees. Phil was one of the men in the group.

> As you share the gospel and you aren't sure whether or not people will ever be saved, remember the two words that change everything in an instance: *but God.*

We were coming up De Soto. On our right was a middle school we had used as our West Valley location for church on Sunday mornings. On our left was a big hospital. At that exact spot, one of the other riders accidentally cut hard into Phil's path and hit him, sending Phil and his bicycle crashing to the ground.

I remember the sound of his hip shattering against the pavement. I remember watching his head slide in front of my wheel. I *barely* missed him. Only by the grace of God did I avoid crashing myself. It happened at lightning speed and yet, strangely, in slow motion.

A few of us stayed with Phil as he lay in the street, screaming and cursing in pain. Since he crashed directly across a busy six-lane street from a hospital, Phil didn't have to wait long to be picked up by an ambulance that promptly took him to the ER. I hung out at the hospital for a few hours until his wife arrived. It turned out Phil would need a hip replacement.

When Phil got out of the hospital, some of us guys from the church started calling him. Just checking in on him and seeing if he was doing okay. We also brought gifts to his home, little things to cheer him up.

Most people would expect that sort of thing. Usually you get gifts or cards when you've been in the hospital. But apparently Phil didn't know about any of that because he could not for the life of him figure out why we were being so nice to him. No one had ever treated him like this before.

Phil is not a Christian. He is Jewish, though he admits he doesn't practice the faith. By looking at us, he and I could not be any more opposite. But we have formed an unlikely friendship, and I do not think I could love him any more than I do.

Phil is a serious guy. He's got a funny side, and if you get to know him well enough you'll be blessed to see it. But by meeting him, you can tell he's seen a lot in his life.

A few months after his accident, Phil started riding with us again. One night we were riding in a group down Winnetka Avenue. As we rode past, Phil pointed out one of the houses to me.

He said to me, "I used to buy drugs in that house."

I laughed out loud. I did not expect him to say that.

"That house too," Phil said, pointing out a second one about a block and a half later. "I used to buy drugs there too."

He told me he had been addicted to drugs for a long time, in and out of rehab. Now he's trying to turn his life around and get healthy again. That's why he started cycling in the first place.

Phil is looking for something. You wouldn't see that immediately. He's got a tough exterior, but he wants to make sense of everything that has happened to him in his life. He wants to figure out what's real and what he believes.

A friend of mine named Frank Sontag hosts his own Christian radio show on KKLA-FM, which is the most-listened-to Christian radio station in the world. Once, while he was on a trip to Israel, Frank asked me to host one of his time slots. Truth be told, I didn't know what I was doing. I was just pressing buttons, hoping I wouldn't break anything!

But I was in the studio, interviewing a guest, and I got a text from Phil. The text read:

> *How is it that I'm setting my clock on my car radio when I accidentally turn to channel 99.5 and hear somebody. It sounds just like you. I say to myself, that sounds just like Dudley and as sure as heck you're on the radio saying, Hi I'm Dudley.*

First of all, the word *heck* in that text surprised me because he usually chooses other words. Let's just say he has a broad vocabulary.

Second, who sets the clock on their car radio anymore?

But it gets better. Guess whom I was interviewing at that exact moment?

A Jewish rabbi named Ron Li-Paz, the head cantor of Valley Outreach Synagogue. Honestly, what are the chances I was speaking to a Jewish rabbi at the very moment Phil was setting the clock on his car radio?

It was then I knew that something important was happening. This wasn't all coincidence. God was at work in Phil's life.

There's more.

"... Yet"

Over the course of our rides, many of the guys in my cycling group had invited Phil to church. He'd never been to church. Never once stepped inside a church building. But one night I got up to preach, and I looked out at the congregation, and wouldn't you know it? Phil was right there—in the front row—sitting next to a young woman I had never met before, whom I later learned was his daughter.

After the service, we all sat down in my office to talk. There was no way I was letting Phil leave the building without finding out how he had gotten there. During our conversation, Phil's daughter shared that she had been in and out rehab. She lived out of town, but while she was in town during the weekend, she wanted to find a church to attend. So Phil brought her to Shepherd Church where I preach! We talked in my office for a while, laughing and crying about the goodness of God bringing us to that moment in time.

There's more.

When I was having some medical issues with my heart, one of the most challenging and difficult points in my life, Phil was one of the first to check in on me to see how I was doing. I got a text message from him one day that was full of concern and disbelief that this was happening to me. He asked how I was, and I tried to assure him that I was going to be okay, even though I wasn't certain myself. Then he wrote, "Wait, am *I* going to have to visit *you* in the hospital for a change?" That made me laugh.

I joked back and ended the text with something like, "God bless you, brother." All jokes aside, I wanted to express my gratitude for him thinking of me.

But then Phil wrote something I did not expect.

He wrote, "Hey, you know I'm not a Christian ... yet."

Let me tell you: every conversation, every prayer, every gift, every meal, and every bike ride I've shared with Phil are all worth that precious possibility that he might someday invite the Lord into his heart. (And even if Phil never gets saved—which I hope is not the case, and by faith I don't believe will be the case—there is no greater honor in this life than to be able to show someone a glimpse of Christ's love and character.) From my friendships with Phil, Dave Hopla, Peggy, and others, to Frank Jenner's brief conversations with strangers and Ewa's talks with Czarek . . . you never know what interaction or relationship you might have with someone that could eventually lead that person to Christ!

The word *yet* compels me.

I pray that you would be compelled too. To respond to a lost and dying world with the hope you have in Jesus. To use the keys you've received to share your faith with confidence and effectiveness. To continue planting seeds, not knowing where they might spring up, but trusting God to bring about a harvest. The possibilities are endless! You have time, opportunities, relationships, and gifts that God has given you to be a light for Him.

You've learned that the steps are not very difficult. But that doesn't mean it won't take persistence and commitment, love and gentleness, boldness and prayer. With the Lord's guidance and the work of the Holy Spirit, put what you've learned into practice—today—and go out into the world with a heart that is compelled to tell others about the new life you've received in Christ Jesus. The new life that can be theirs too. Let's get this party started!

DISCUSSION QUESTIONS

1. Are there any people in your life who came to know Christ, even though you thought they would never give their lives over to Him? How did God get ahold of their hearts, despite your doubts?

2. When you think about how God worked behind the scenes in my friend Phil's life (see page 218), who in your life do you see God similarly bringing to a place of receiving Christ?

3. Who are some of your friends, family members, and coworkers who do not know Jesus yet . . . especially individuals or family members whom you can never see surrendering their lives to Christ?

4. Keep this list of names with you and read through them every day. Pray for God to reach them and bring them to His loving embrace. Pray for their hearts to be softened to His love and grace, and to give them a desire to be loved by God.

5. Pray right now that God would give you the opportunity and courage to share the truth with them.

6. How does 1 Corinthians 15:56–58 give you hope for victory, despite the mortality of our bodies and the struggles we face in this life?

Acknowledgments

I regard evangelism as the most important thing we have been called to do as followers of Christ. We were saved so that we might help others to be saved. We were led to Christ so that we might lead others to Christ. The testimony of God's grace in our lives becomes the compelling reason to tell others of Jesus's gift of salvation, which is readily available to all who believe.

Many people told us that books on evangelism weren't popular any more—that we were wasting our time on such a topic. Knowing the importance of the Great Commission, as stated in Matthew 28:18–20, and knowing that there are those who feel this topic is no longer valid, I had no choice but to write a book about the greatest calling on earth: to tell others of the good news of Jesus Christ.

This book has been a labor of love, more than ten long years in the making. Those involved in *Compelled* coming to fruition deserve a medal for their work and perseverance.

There are many people I want to thank for coming alongside me to make this book possible. First, I'd like to thank my wife, Renee, and our children for their constant love and support. It is a joy to go through life with such an amazing family that honors me by honoring the Lord. Second, I must thank my executive pastor, Tim Winters, who faithfully and wisely runs the operations of Shepherd Church. Tim does the job of at least seven people, and he has been both a loyal friend and a true brother. I hope his Cardinals win another World Series in the near future to reward him for his faithfulness to me.

My sincerest thanks to my writing assistant, Angie Merrill, the one person who has been there from the start of this journey, helping me to bring this book to completion—and with every draft, bringing a fierce determination to see the burden of my heart realized in print. She is like a master artist who skillfully paints and turns into reality my thoughts and ideas. Without her, this book would have never seen the light of day. I am forever indebted to her, not just for her work ethic, but also for her true love and passion for this project from the first word to the last.

Thank you to Kyle Welch for lending his sharp research and editing skills. I've said before that Kyle is the smartest person I know, and yet he serves with such humility and grace.

Many thanks to my agent, Don Gates, for championing this book and being my advocate. Don is a wise and dedicated gentleman who firmly believed in this project.

To the team at Worthy Publishing—editors Kyle Olund and Leeanna Nelson, Nicole Pavlas, Caroline Green, the copyeditor, proofreaders, and graphic designers, and Jeana Ledbetter and Byron Williamson, who lead this fine group of people—thank you for all your hard work in helping to make this book a reality. You can take the rest of the week off. :)

Last, but not least, my love and regards to my earthly father, H. Dean Rutherford, for instilling in me a deep sense of compassion to see the lost saved. His example and preaching stirred my heart and taught me how to weep over those who do not know Jesus.

Scriptures to Memorize

Make a photocopy of the following scriptures or simply cut them out and place them in your home, office, car, or anywhere you are likely to see them regularly. Memorizing these Bible verses is very helpful in explaining our need for salvation and leading someone to put his or her trust in Jesus Christ.

For God so loved the world that he gave
his one and only Son, that whoever believes in him
shall not perish but have eternal life.
John 3:16

Jesus answered, "I am the way and the truth and the life.
No one comes to the Father except through me."
John 14:6

Salvation is found in no one else,
for there is no other name under heaven
given to mankind by which we must be saved.
Acts 4:12

For it is by grace you have been saved, through faith—
and this is not from yourselves, it is the gift of God—
not by works, so that no one can boast.
Ephesians 2:8–9

For there is one God and one mediator between
God and mankind, the man Christ Jesus,
who gave himself as a ransom for all people.
1 Timothy 2:5–6

For all have sinned and fall short of the glory of God.
Romans 3:23

For the wages of sin is death, but the gift of God
is eternal life in Christ Jesus our Lord.
Romans 6:23

But God demonstrates his own love for us in this:
While we were still sinners, Christ died for us.
Romans 5:8

If you declare with your mouth, "Jesus is Lord,"
and believe in your heart that God
raised him from the dead, you will be saved.
Romans 10:9

We were therefore buried with him through
baptism into death in order that,
just as Christ was raised from the dead through
the glory of the Father, we too may live a new life.
Romans 6:4

Notes

Chapter 1

1. "Growth of the World's Population," www.english-online.at/.

2. *Strong's Exhaustive Concordance, #29.*

3. www.dictionary.com.

4. http://www.operationworld.org/hidden/evangelical-population

Chapter 2

1. "Dave Hopla Biography," Hoop Group (September 1, 2015), www.hoopgroup.com.

2. *Strong's Exhaustive Concordance, #2537.*

3. "Missions and Evanglism Quotes," www.tentmaker.org.

4. 2 Corinthians 5:18.

5. www.davehopla.com.

Chapter 3

1. "Manny Pacquiao Interview at Shepherd Church" (April 28, 2015), www.youtube.com/dudleyrutherford.

2. *Manny*, Gravitas Ventures (2015), www.mannypacquiaomovie.com.

3. "The Market for Self-Improvement Products & Services," CISION PR Newswire (January 20, 2015), www.prnewswire.com/news-releases/the-market-for-self-improvement-products--services-289121641.html.

4. Rhonda Byrne, *The Secret* (New York: Atria Books, 2006, 2016), 59.

5. Ruchi Singh, "My Own Genie," Living Stories (posted July 18, 2015), www.thesecret.tv.

6. John Gravois, "Think Negative!," *Slate* (May 16, 2007), www.slate.com.

Chapter 4

1. "The Death of Mr. Eternity—Arthur Stace," www.historychannel.com/au.

2. Genesis 9:16.

3. Psalms 41:13.

4. 1 Timothy 1:17.

5. Revelation 1:11.

6. Ephesians 3:11.

7. "World Birth and Death Rates," Ecology (2011), www.ecology.com.

8. Matthew 8:12; 13:42, 50; 22:13; 24:51; 25:30; Luke 13:28.

9. 1 Thessalonians 4:16.

Chapter 5

1. Greg Laurie, "The Value of a Soul," www.oneplace.com.

2. Billy Graham, "The Value of Your Soul," *Decision Magazine* (July 28, 2012), www.billygraham.org.

3. "Bible Animals: Sheep," Bible History Online, www.bible-history.com.

4. "Maya Angelou: Her Life and Accomplishments," *USA Today* (May 28, 2014), www
.usatoday.com.

Chapter 6

1. Richard Klein, "Profiles in Prayer: Praying John Hyde," www.cbn.com.

2. *Strong's Exhaustive Concordance*, #1411.

Chapter 7

1. 2 Timothy 2:4.

2. Acts 8:30.

3. Acts 8:34.

Chapter 8

1. Russell Moore, "The Next Billy Graham Might Be Drunk Right Now" (January 2, 2012),
www.russellmoore.com.

Chapter 10

1. Dallas Willard, "Spiritual Formation in Christ for the Whole Life and Whole Person,"
Vocatio, vol. 12, no. 2 (Spring 2001), 7.

2. "5 Reasons Why We Should Study God's Word" (May 4, 2015), www.biblestudytools.com.

3. "Short-Term Memory," McGill University, http://thebrain.mcgill.ca/flash/d/d_07/d_07
_cr/d_07_cr_tra/d_07_cr_tra.html.

4. David Jeremiah, "Becoming a Christian," Turning Point, www.davidjeremiah.org.

Chapter 11

1. Hugo Martín, "After Dark, the Dirty Work at Disneyland Begins," *LA Times* (May 2,
2010), www.latimes.com.

2. William Lane Craig, *On Guard: Defending Your Faith with Reason and Precision* (Colorado
Springs: David C. Cook, 2010), 18.

Chapter 12

1. "Ostracism More Damaging than Bullying in the Workplace," UBC News, University of
British Columbia, May 29, 2014.

2. Matthew D. Lieberman, *Social: Why Our Brains Are Wired to Connect* (New York: Crown,
2013), 59.

3. Genesis 37:1–36.

4. *Pocket Oxford Classical Greek Dictionary*, eds James Morwood and John Taylor (New York:
Oxford University Press, 2002).

5. Frank Raj, "Gandhi Glimpsed Christ, Rejecting Christianity as a False Religion,"
Washington Times (December 14, 2014), www.washingtontimes.com.

6. A 1926 review by the Reverend W. P. King (then pastor of the First Methodist Church of Gainesville, Georgia) of E. Stanley Jones's *The Christ of the Indian Road* (New York: Abington Press, 1925).

7. Dibin Samuel, "Mahatma Gandhi and Christianity," *Christianity Today* (August 14, 2008), www.christiantoday.co.in.

8. http://censusindia.gov.in/Census_And_You/religion.aspx.

9. "Trivia & Facts," iditarod.com

Chapter 13

1. "Nigeria: Habila Shot for Refusing to Deny Jesus," The Voice of the Martyrs, www.youtube.com/vomcanada.

2. Kelly Shackelford, ed., *Undeniable: The Survey of Hostility to Religion in America* (Plano, TX: Liberty Institute, 2014), 9.

3. Ibid., 5–6.

4. Ibid., 4.

5. Scott Dolan, "Man Found Dead in Portland Apartment Had Been Beaten, Kicked to Death," *Portland Press Herald* (August 24, 2015).

6. Anthony J. Saldarini, "Sanhedrin," *Harper Collins Bible Dictionary*, ed. Paul J. Achtemeier (San Francisco: HarperCollins, 1996), 971–72.

7. George Thomas, "Secret Worship: N. Korea Defector Tells of Survival," CBN News (August 6, 2015), www.cbn.com.

8. Monica Cantilero, "Defector Reveals Life in North Korea, 'The Most Dangerous Place to Be a Christian,'" *Christianity Today* (August 12, 2015), www.christianitytoday.com.

Chapter 14

1. "The George Street Evangelist," and www.divinerevelations.info.

2. Ray C. Stedman, "Man of Faith," *Christianity Today*, vol. 30, no. 5, http://www.preachingtoday.com/illustrations/1997/december/982.html.

About Dudley Rutherford

Dudley Rutherford is the senior pastor of Shepherd Church, a 15,000-member congregation. Through the Lift Up Jesus television ministry, Pastor Dudley's sermons are broadcast on TV and radio nationwide. He is the founder of DreamofDestiny.org, a ministry designed to foster ethnic diversity within the Christian Church. He is the author of *Walls Fall Down, God Has an App for That, Unleashed, Romancing Royalty,* and *Proverbs in a Haystack.* He has had the distinction of speaking for several professional sports teams and has been a featured chapel speaker for the World Series. Dudley earned his bachelor's degree from Ozark Christian College and his master's degree in church growth from Hope International University. He also obtained an honorary Doctorate of Divinity from St. Charles University. Dudley and his beautiful wife, Renee, have three children and reside in Porter Ranch, CA.